PARENTING MANTRAS

7 STEPS TO WORRYING LESS
& LOVING MORE

RIDHI DOONGURSEE

ISBN 978-93-81115-78-7

Cover Design: Fravashi Aga
Printed in India by Nutech Print Services - India.

This edition is reprinted in 2018.

Published in 2013

An imprint of
LEADSTART PUBLISHING PVT LTD

Unit 25, Building A/1Near Wadala RTO,
Wadala (East), Mumbai 400037, INDIA
T + 91 96 99933000 E info@leadstartcorp.com
W www.leadstartcorp.com

Marketed & Distributed by:

A Division of
Bennett Coleman & Co. Ltd.

The Times of India, 10 Daryaganj, New Delhi 110002
Phone: 011-39843333 Email: tgb@timesgroup.in,
www.toibooks.com

To my darling son.
And for the incredible love and joy
that parents feel for and receive
from their children.

ABOUT THE AUTHOR

RIDHI DOONGURSEE graduated from the University of Warwick, UK, and then did a stint in Banking before deciding to follow her entrepreneurial dream. Ridhi has spent over five years extensively studying and researching the concept of parenting. She is a mother herself and many of her insights come from her personal hands-on experiences with her son. In the course of her research and her life's lessons, Ridhi discovered certain *mantras* that can truly help parents make the most of their time with their children. Being a voracious reader who believes in constantly unlearning and relearning, she wanted to write a book on these discoveries – on how to *love* every minute of being a parent; how to be happy yourself; and how to raise happy children, and so share her learnings with the many, many parents out there who love and struggle to do their best as parents.

Ridhi resides in Mumbai, India, and can be reached at: ridhidoongursee@gmail.com

CONTENTS

INTRODUCTION

You don't really understand human nature unless you know why a child on a merry-go-round will wave at his parents every time around – and why his parents will always wave back.
~ William D. Tammeus

Parenting can be more joyful than the most beautiful childhood memory. These pages are my account of what works to totally and completely dispel the panic attack of, 'Oh god! How am I going to raise a baby?' and make you love being a parent instead. This book is certainly not about what any religion says about the way we should bring up children. Nor is it the psychologist's perspective. It is written from the point of view of a mother who has been to many seminars, courses, read oh-so-many books, and realized through experience, the 7 critical and magical steps to happy parenting. If you are thinking of having a baby or already have one on the way, and are worried about parenting being stressful, follow these steps and I can assure you it will make you feel like a good parent, a happy parent and raise children who know you love them.

I wasn't always a mother. Neither is anyone. All new moms and dads learn the ropes in their own way. On a daily basis, I would be asked questions like: *How are you so calm with your child?* /*How does your son sit and enjoy meals on a table full of adults and eat the same meal? /How do you manage to balance your professional life, your role as a mother, and your social life?* Yes, it felt good now but I'll be honest, I had attended many parenting seminars, taken month-long courses and read a gazillion books, to figure out what works and how to get that Zen. I know many mothers go through the same drill. The only thing I perhaps did differently was to take the positive aspects of whatever I exposed myself to and picked and chose what seemed most logical to me. At no point did I get harried about trying to implement every single strategy I was told about.

In the many seminars I attended and was inspired by, there were some genius concepts explained, but they also focused a lot on academics and theory – from 'how to get your three-year old to start reading' and 'ways to get your fifteen-day old baby to crawl' to 'how to appropriately use flash and dot cards to help your child understand complicated calculations by the age of four'. And they sound great, I agree. These teachings were the reason I, and many others, signed up in the first place. But at the end of the tenure, what stayed with me were the parts that promoted happiness, which I have, based on my experiences, elaborated on in this book. The fact that they corresponded with the reason we become parents in the first place – to experience limitless joy – only helped strengthen my beliefs even more.

In this book I have focused my energies on explaining certain concepts that worked like magic! The things I was looking for in my parent-child relationship. Over time, I began noticing a difference in my parenting style. I had somehow become transformed. Narrating my experiences seemed to help other young parents to deal with some of the serious issues they were facing as parents. That's when I felt that I wanted to share this 'way of life' which I had adopted wholeheartedly. The intention is to introduce you to the euphoria of being a mom or dad. I hope you thoroughly enjoy reading the book. I love being a mother, and have attempted to iron out some of the issues that are usually related to parenting, so you can experience the pleasures of this journey.

Do you want to truly love every minute of parenting? Shift your focus from the question, *Am I doing enough*? to the thought, *I feel so complete with the beautiful bond I share with my child*. Do not worry about, *Is my child at par with the other kids?* and start believing, *I am so lucky to have such an intelligent and unique child*.

Happy parents bring up happy children. In our modern times, parenting seems to have become very stressful and competitive. The natural beauty of it is disappearing. So I wanted to write a light-hearted, helpful book – a guide that could help people feel like good parents; a diary of sorts that would give them the strength to believe that they were doing their best for their children; and a story that would convince them that their children really are perfect and unique beings. Each child is a genius.

A good book can change your life. *The Secret* by Rhonda Byrne and *You Can Heal Your Life* by Louise Hay, irrevocably altered mine. Books have the power to spark a series of beautiful thoughts within you. The books mentioned above, taught me some things that have now become the basis on which I lead my life – positivity, gratitude, love for others and for ourselves. Various cultures have been imparting this know-how in subtle doses for ages. But these books make the concepts seem more logical and based on pure understanding. During my years-long self-help quest, I kept looking for the one book on parenting that would contain the ideas for 100 % happy parenting. But after reading a fair amount, I realized that there wasn't any simple and easy-to-read book that encompasses some simple, life-changing tips.

All the information in this book has come from years of reading, learning and unlearning. I left no stone (in this case, no page), unturned, to gain knowledge about parenting and children. I wanted to share all those thoughts – the many things I learnt, the experiences and the good advice (which despite common perception, was sometimes very useful), and the bad. Most importantly, I wanted to share the spiritual, mental, and emotional learning from this beautiful, confusing and sometimes intimidating experience.

I hope this book helps you to sit down, smell the daisies, and just focus your energies on the bond you share with your child. If I can make every reader smile a little more and stress a lot less, my wish would have been fulfilled. So, dear parents, this is for you, for parents-to-be, and even grandparents and other primary caretakers. I hope this book will help your child grow up to be a happy, healthy adult who shares a beautiful bond with people, communicates well, and is loving and confident. It will make you feel like a complete person and a good parent! It doesn't matter if you're a working dad or mom, a stay-at-home mom, an over-involved mom, or under or over-involved father – all of you will be able to relate to this book.

Though I have enumerated a few tips on how to develop a child's academic and physical intelligence, the focus of the book is on emotional, spiritual, and social intelligence. Somehow, in today's competitive world, those three parts have been sidelined today. At the end of some chapters, I have put down some happiness tips, which will allow readers to get an overview of each section. But before you begin reading, spend a little time doing some introspection. For instance, as a parent, there are certain important things you want for your children: you want them to be happy and healthy, and you hope they are caring and have a fulfilling life with achievements they can be proud of and fulfilled by. You also want them to have healthy adult relationships.

Now what do we want from our children?

- Their love
- Their respect
- Their occasional appreciation

And what do we want to provide our child with?

- A happy childhood
- Opportunities to have the best life
- Security

This book will leave you feeling comfortable and certain that you will achieve all of the above from your relationship with your child. The techniques mentioned in the following chapters work especially well during the first few years of a child's life. They will continue to work even after that, but it may take a little longer to achieve the desired results. That is because, after a certain age, children tend to develop patterns that are difficult to undo.

Over time, the older and stricter methods of parenting have also changed. They worked well years ago, but as we have evolved we have designed methods that work better for each new generation. The tools I have mentioned in this book have worked wonders for me and for many other parents who share these beliefs and philosophies. Believe that this journey is enjoyable and it will be so. You want the child of your dreams? You can have one. You want a unique, gifted and gentle-natured baby? You will have one. You want to fix certain doubts you have in your mind? Absolutely! You want to have perfect communication with your children? It will happen, I assure you. Set off on this journey with me with an open mind, follow these steps and whatever you have always wanted your parenting experience to be, will magically come true. With this book I want to rid you of your worries and introduce you to the greatest joyride in life – parenting.

STEP 1
BECOMING A PARENT IS THE BIGGEST DECISION OF YOUR LIFE ~ WHAT YOU WISH YOU KNEW

Be prepared, it's the real deal! Here are the things we all want to know when we first get pregnant.

THE BIG DECISION

Are we ready to be parents?

Making a decision to have a child – it's momentous. It is to decide forever to have your heart go walking around outside your body. ~ Elizabeth Stone

Trust me, if there's anything that can turn your world upside-down and inside-out at the same time and make you smile till your face hurts, it's the decision to bring a bundle of joy into this world. When you're making a life-changing decision like becoming parents, some optimistic but unrealistic people, in an attempt to convince you, will say, 'How much could things possibly change?' Yeah, well those guys haven't had kids for sure. They also haven't experienced heaven up-close and personal like I have and I continue to. I got married quite early. I had just moved in with this man whom I adored and the closest I came to thinking about having a baby was listening to Justin Bieber's hit track playing full blast in my gym. I was stubborn, looking forward to my career, and far from ready to take on the big job of parenting.

I knew at that point that once I had a child, I would have to become responsible for life. I would always have him/her on my mind. No matter where I was travelling or if I was in the world's best nightclub, grooving next to Paris Hilton, I would still be thinking of whether my baby was okay. But then, one morning, something changed (it really was that dramatic). I suddenly found myself feeling prepared or at least inching towards that desire, faster than usual. Many days were spent having those mandatory yet lengthy discussions with family members (*Yes! Please have a child soon; we're dying to be grandparents*), and friends (*Oh my god! Are you really ready? Wow!*). Even more time was spent asking ourselves the imperative questions. Are we financially ready? Are we prepared to make the lifestyle changes? Would we have to move into a bigger house? Was there job security? Would we be able to give our angel the best upbringing at this stage?

But suddenly, even mundane situations began turning in favor of the big decision. Our work, for instance, was going to keep us from travelling for two years. And this seemed like the perfect timeframe for us to become parents and take care of our newborn without the worry of having to jet off somewhere. We realized that we had travelled extensively, partied through many nights, and slogged at work for even more days. It was time to take our relationship to the next level. And it was around then that I felt sure that I wanted to live the greatest experience a woman can have in life. That's when I knew we were ready for the two big Ps – pregnancy and parenthood!

Many modern couples are too scared to have children. They see today's stressed parents who look like they have such difficult lives! Really? Since when did a joyful experience like parenting become scary? Since when did a blessing become a fear? Well it doesn't need to be. Here are some tools that will help you enjoy this joyride.

At this time

1. There's no such thing as too much information. Utilize all the numerous resources available to you – online articles, baby courses, videos, and books – to make this natural journey even more fun.

2. Don't stress. Having a child comes naturally to a woman. Your body works like magic to protect your baby and prepare you for this experience. Your system will go through innumerable changes to ready itself for your child. So if you're worried about whether you'll be a good mother or if you'll be able to wake up when your baby cries, don't! You're not alone in this. Thousands of years of evolution and mother nature are part of your support system. Human beings are meant to procreate. It is, in many ways, their purpose and responsibility towards mankind.

WE ARE PREGNANT!

Those nine bittersweet months

This doesn't happen often. So, first of all, enjoy every second of it. For once, you're actually hoping to get knocked up after having some mind-blowingly great unprotected intercourse (I like the scientific ring to that term). The fact that you know this session means so much more than all the others, adds to the ecstasy. Every month, a few days before I was supposed to start my period, I'd run and get myself a few pregnancy tests (safety in numbers if you ask me). Month one, you usually emerge from the bathroom disappointed. I did, for a couple of reasons actually. First, for all those years I had been paranoid about missing my period because birth control promised only 98 % safety; and now, when I want to make it to that niche group of mothers, the Universe was making me wait! But on second thoughts, thank God for that. We don't want that much fertility around the world, do we?

Then on one of those unexpected evenings when I had finally succeeded in distracting myself from my yet-to-be-conceived child, there it was. The pregnancy test that I religiously carried out and left at the bathroom counter had taken an extra minute to let the second blessed line emerge! And there it was. My one-way ticket to awesomeness – parenthood! I was pretty sure I heard fireworks, but that could also have been the neighborhood kids. But the feeling, the best in the whole wide world, was best defined as indescribable! This is my favorite quote for this phase:

A child gives birth to a mother. ~ Unknown

For the first few weeks, you want to imagine the first signs of your baby bump. You also want to make the most of the privileges of being pregnant. But the most exciting part of this initial phase is your first sonography. I remember we were running late for the appointment and my husband, the loving, law-abiding citizen that he is, actually skipped a traffic signal. A minute later, a police officer caught us red-handed, sneaking past. "My pregnant wife has a doctor's appointment we're late for," said my husband, genuinely trying to reason with the cop, who after a glance at my non-existent belly, must have thought to himself, 'The excuses these kids come up with these days!'. But we looked concerned enough, thankfully, so he let us go with a strict warning. I saw it as a good sign – the pregnancy was not only meddling with my hormones, but my husband's too! I was not alone.

With each subsequent visit to the gynaecologist, you marvel at nature even more. I was barely six weeks into my pregnancy when I heard my child's heartbeat for the first time at the clinic. There's nothing that can be equated with that moment. Eventually you can see hands and legs and each doctor's visit is so exciting. I was carrying life inside me. That fuzzy black and white image of the inside of my womb was *my* little baby. With the mood swings and cravings kicking in, the highlight of each month was looking forward to the next sonography. In-between, I decided I'd educate myself about everything there was to learn about pregnancy. Yes, you can actually read about which part of the baby's body is developing on the 60th day. Please do refer to Step 2: Think It. Get It! It will be helpful at this stage for both moms and dads.

Anyway, between Lamaze (breathing exercises), Kegels (vaginal exercises), long walks, and lots of books, I was (and you will be too), ready in theory for the real deal.

Tips I think are lifesavers

1. Get pampered. It is extremely important moms and dads, that you spoil yourself during those nine months. You need to love yourself to be able to love your child. Take time out for a long bath or a spa session. Work on feeling good, taking a holiday, and spending money on yourself. Don't think about whether you will have enough cash to buy your baby toys. Children enjoy playing with empty boxes just as much!
2. Enjoy the attention. Very soon, you will have enough and more on your plate to handle.
3. Talk to other families. Nothing works like some first-hand experiential motivation. Take time out for a friendly chat with your best friend or mother.
4. Exercise. Don't take those doctor-recommended regimens lightly. Make sure you do the pregnancy stretches and breathing exercises, and walk as much as possible. All this comes in handy when you're ready to push. Even husband and wife strolls are great for health, emotionally and physically.
5. Enjoy your baby photos. I've said it before and I'll say it again, nothing compares to the joy of being able to see the shape of your angel on that sonography machine. Let the maternal instincts kick in!
6. Don't let people stress you out. Listen to what you feel like, and ignore the rest. Eat healthy, allowing yourself to enjoy munching on what you love best. Don't get influenced by those who are negative or constantly stressed.

THE BIRTH AND THEREAFTER

The First Month as Mom 'n Dad

Before you were conceived I wanted you. Before you were born I loved you. Before you were here an hour I would die for you.

~ Maureen Hawkins

The last 30 days of your pregnancy are the toughest simply because you're more or less out of patience. And you don't have any more sonographies to look forward to. At this point, I just wanted to drive up to the hospital and start pushing! Eventually I did. Those 12 hours of labour pains taught me to take advice from only the most reliable sources in life, and especially when it comes to the epidural – just take it! I was advised to avoid the epidural by a well meaning doctor and a friend. However, after those long hours of excruciating labour pains, I was told that it was medically necessary to take it as the pain was not allowing me to dilate further. I gave birth to my little boy within 30 minutes of the angelic shot! (Refer to Step 6: Filter The World. It's a very important reference point for the constant advice that will come your way.)

There he was, snuggling up next to me like he'd been doing so for ages. As for the delivery, I said it then and I'll say it again, it felt beyond magical, and I would do it many times over without blinking an eyelid. The next three days felt like they lasted a year. Or at least I wanted them to. Those hours with my child were the most divine moments of my being. We felt emotion like never before. We gazed into our newest family member's eyes as he slowly wrapped his tiny hand around our fingers. I thought I knew my husband's every look, but he too, on that day, glowed brighter than ever. The connection that children have with the distinct scent of their mothers is something that even science has proved. So basically the minute they come into the arms of their parents, babies feel and look at peace. Being able to watch him/her calm down when you hold them is an unbelievable experience, you will love it and feel so proud. Enjoy this lovely time.

This is also when you realize that if there's anything that's free in life, it's advice (again, please refer to Step 6: Filter the World). Although some of it was really useful, you have to filter through to what works with your parenting philosophy. At times, experience counts, but at other times you have to combine old-school and new-age options to get your perfect fix.

At the end of the first few weeks, changing diapers will be like second nature to you. I think my husband and I could have done it in our sleep (I'm sure we did too). But more importantly, I understood one thing – babies cry. Yes, they do. That's the only way they know how to communicate. Whether it's an uncomfortable posture that's troubling them or a nappy change is in order, or when they are ready for their next meal, all a baby has to do is break into a sniffle, and parents know exactly what they want. Try to form a routine so that they are well fed and well rested and reasons to cry are reduced. But trust me, whatever you try, they *will* cry, so don't beat yourself up over it. As time passes, you will be able to recognize the cries and their specific causes – whether its hunger or gas or just time to fall sleep.

My husband I were each other's support system through this time. So don't hesitate to just stop whatever you're doing and give the man you love a big hug, for no reason. Trust me, it works wonders for both of you. Remember, the father might not have carried the child for nine months, but he also goes through phases of uncertainty and insecurity. In moments like that, I would just remind him that I was with him in this, and together, we would give our family the best upbringing ever. You will also realize it's not just the dad and mom in this. Somehow, when the mom is the one supposed to be dealing with the hormonal upheavals in her body, everyone else around her also feels it is their right to comment and interfere in the smallest things, when all they should be doing is giving unconditional support and love to the new parents.

Take it from me, a mother's instincts (further detailed in Step 7), are rarely wrong, and if you feel someone around you is being negative or hurtful, just distance yourself from that person. You and your body have been through enough! The first few weeks just seem like long, long sleepless nights. But trust me, they will pass. The coming months will be easier. Within some time, your baby will start holding up his/her head. You have no idea what a big feat that is. By which time, the feeding and sleeping patterns will more or less be in place. Your life will start getting back to a semi-normal state. Also, if you apply the theories detailed later in this book, the so-called difficult children or phases of parenting which you hear about, will never happen!

During this time the trick is to try and sync your day with your baby's. I rested when my son slept, and I gave myself some 'alone-time' when my parents and in-laws were around to keep him entertained. You have to steal a liitle time in the middle of everything for yourself and your husband. Give him a lot of affection as and when you can and don't forget he's still getting used to not having all your attention. Basically, by the end of the first 30 days, you're at the peak of your energy and exhaustion combined. You can multitask like a dream – be it changing diapers, making your baby giggle, giving him/her a soothing massage, changing or bathing your baby despite the sleep deprivation. And that's it. Before you know it, you're supermom!

Between the liquid feeding, breast-feeding, some poop, a little burping, lots of pee-pee, some more poop, many more nappies (many, many more nappies actually), you will be baptized by fire. Soon the firsts begin – the first responsive smile, the first finger clenching, the first coos. You have to experience them to believe what it feels like. It gives your life purpose like never before. It makes you smile and cry for little known reasons, and do you feel zest for life or what! From then on, I knew my son would be the reason behind every move I made and I was prepared and looking forward to every minute. My bundle of joy was wrapped in my arms and I in my husband's. The journey had begun.

Important pointers especially for this phase

1. Hold your child. Soon after you've delivered, hug your baby close to your body – it's a beautiful bonding moment.
2. Don't be afraid to top feed. It takes a day or two for the breast milk to come in, and unless you want to deal with a hungry, crying newborn for the first two days/nights, just give a top feed once or twice while

you're in hospital. Your child will not reject your breast milk once you start on that, and you will get some much-needed sleep. I did this when I delivered. After the first few days, I started breast-feeding. Various people gave me far too many opinions on the matter. Some said, *Exclusive breast feeding is important on the first few days*, while others claimed, *The baby will have to deal with nipple confusion*, and so on. Nothing of the sort happened. When I spoke to a few doctors, I realized that this is standard practice for moms who also want to breast feed exclusively. Of course, you still put the baby to your breast, as *colostrum* (which comes before full milk flow), is very good for the child.

3. Get a breast pump. It makes life easier and reduces your discomfort. Also, definitely learn the 'correct' way to feed, unless you want to be in agony while your child is busy getting a dose of nutrients. Your nurse, pediatrician, or gynecologist can teach you how.
4. Feeling like your body's taking time to produce milk? See a doctor. Don't worry. There are many natural remedies (Satavarex, and some even say, Guinness), that help increase milk flow.
5. Avoid the scar. The vaccinations that leave those round marks on children's arms can be given at the base of their feet now. This should be confirmed with your doctor, of course.
6. Newborns lose hair. It's natural. Their bodies are at the healthiest stage, and new hair will grow back as soon as the old batch falls.
7. Buy a baby bath chair. It is a soft net chair in which your baby lies so you can bathe him/her easily. Once you are home and the nurses are not around with their pro

techniques, this goes a long way in helping to hold your tiny baby in the wet conditions of a baby's bath (specific instructions will be given by your nurse for this).

8. At night, some babies sleep for three to four hours at a stretch, some wake up every hour or two for a feed. If you want to sleep longer, consider expressing once in the middle just after a feed so that your partner or someone who can help give your baby the next feed, and you can get a few more hours of sleep. Also, you or your partner can sleep in separate rooms a few days a week so that both of you take turns with sleeping a little longer if your baby is waking up often.
9. It gets easier. Life gets better after the first 40 days. The sleepless nights subside, and your body starts adjusting to the new world of parenthood. In a matter of three months, you'll be a pro! The first 30 days really are the hardest because the mother has hormonal changes; sleep deprivation and the new feeling of immense responsibility for a life. Trust me, it gets easier, much easier, after the first 30-40 days, and even easier as the baby holds up his/her head in the next three months.

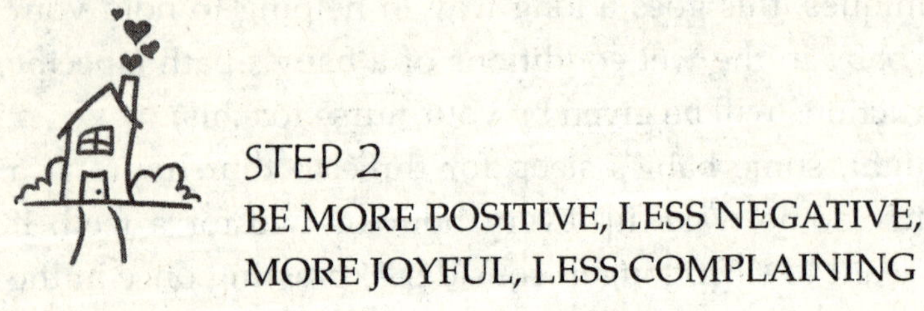

STEP 2
BE MORE POSITIVE, LESS NEGATIVE, MORE JOYFUL, LESS COMPLAINING

THINK IT. GET IT!

Envisioning – Power of the Mind

And, when you want something, all the universe conspires in helping you to achieve it. ~ Paul Coelho

This is something that worked for me during and even after my pregnancy. After the ecstasy of being pregnant settles, one thought enters the mind: 'Nine months later, I'll have to push something the size of a football out of a slot that's currently the size of a keyhole'. Ouch, right?

Those months before and after the delivery, are full of numerous thoughts. Most make you smile, but many also make you wonder. But you have a super power that you should know you have – the ability to make a choice. And not just any choice, but one to ensure you embrace ideas that envision positivity and happiness around you, because that is what you pass on to your child from the beginning. The saying, *What you think is what you get*, has been around for ages. In fact, I am reminded of Albert Einstein. As children, we all remember being told that we only use a fragment of what our minds are capable of. Even a genius like Einstein used just 4 % of his brain during his lifetime, and let's face it, even though this percentage may currently be a matter of debate, he was a pretty smart guy! Now what intrigues me is the other 96%. There is not a molecule in our body that is not being put to use in some manner or the other. That 96% can't possibly be doing nothing. I believe it plays a role – a leading part. It takes the thoughts of the 4% and helps transform them into reality. What we think and focus on is what we get. It may seem far-fetched right now, but this science, like many others domains of knowledge, has yet to be fully analyzed and understood.

The same thought is reflected in the book, *The Secret*. It states that, like the law of gravity (what goes up must come down), there is the law of attraction, wherein you can attract an objective towards your by thinking about it. That's another reason why I love books! Whether it's through inspiring stories or insightful experiences, nothing works the subconscious mind like some good old heart-warming literature. But I truly understood what this meant only after I discovered I was going to be a mommy.

I realized that negativity encourages negativity and positivity attracts positivity. That's why I refused to let myself fall prey to evil thoughts such as, 'I don't want an aggressive child', or 'I don't want to get into an accident', or 'Will I be able to do enough for my baby?'. Sometimes, negative thoughts are enticing and pop up unintentionally. But once you see the effect positive thoughts have on your life, you will automatically avoid negativity like the plague. Like Louise Hay says, *The power is in your current thought*. That's all that matters. Try to be positive in this moment, and the rest will be taken care of.

The subconscious mind is a lot more powerful than we know. When I was expecting my son, the only form of communication that I truly knew was taking place between us was subconscious. Then why on earth would I subject my few-months-old angel to bad thoughts, when he did not even know what the word 'communication' meant. It has five syllables, for heaven's sake! All parents worry. It's natural. It's love that causes the concern, which brings with it some amount of paranoia and stress. So just start telling yourself (you can say it out loud if you feel that works better): *happy thoughts foster happy moments*.

My life experiences have proven this theory to me time and again. And the best way to understand this would be to implement it and watch it change not only your life, but also the lives of those around you. You can improve your life, your pregnancy, and your baby, just by using the energy of your positive thoughts. Envision the holistic attributes, sentiments and abilities you'd like your child to be born with. For instance, if you want your baby to be a supermodel when he/she grows up, wish for your child to achieve boundless recognition and satisfaction from whatever he/she does in life. Basically, whichever qualities you want in your child, focus on them and send out clear signals to the Universe in the form of positive thoughts and energy. The rest, as they say, will all fall into place. What career he/she decides on is a decision only time can tell, but at least you've let the Universe know what you want for your little one is just loads and loads of glee.

You can start sending out messages into the cosmos for your baby early in your pregnancy. You could start with picturing your child (in your mind), how you would want him/her to look and continue seeing those positive attributes all the time you can feel the child growing within you. When I began planning my nine months, I started surrounding myself with cute pictures of what I'd like my child to look like. What happened afterwards, may be, and probably, is a complete coincidence. But what's the harm in learning a life lesson? I always found dimples adorable and even though I never actively expected my baby to be born with the cute dent, guess what, every time my baby smiles now, the dimple at the tip of his nose reminds me to believe in what initially felt so unbelievable.

At the same time, remember that the brain is a wonderfully powerful tool and what our greatly loved superhero Spiderman was told: *With great power, comes great responsibility*, is true in our own case as well. Try to steer clear from disturbing imagery of any sort. The trick, literally, is to *see* the positive attributes you want in your child, and you will see them come to be. The most enjoyable way of doing this is by actually maintaining a compilation of all that imagery in a vision book. Save words, pictures, and thoughts revolving around your child, and make it a point to refer to them regularly just so you can continue maintaining your focus on the positives.

Another success story is that of my sister. She, like many mothers these days, had everyone around her a little worried because she was a few years older than I was when I took on the role of mom. But at no time during those months did she ever let stressful thoughts get to her. She smiled, she asked the Universe for a healthy child.

And on D-day, within 60 minutes, there she was – my niece, wailing away at the taste of adulterated oxygen. If you feel this isn't evidence of 'thinking happy, being happy' theory, know that a few years later, she gave her daughter the greatest present in the world – a sibling. The second time was even easier. She took all of 30 minutes to get her out there! As fantastical as this may feel, and I really like to keep it sounding that way, there is a limitless and untapped source of power that your mind houses and which is at your command. If it has been proved beneficial in various walks of life, professional or romantic, then why not put it to use for our newborns? After all, once you've experienced motherhood, nothing makes you tick like the gentle touch of those soft hands at the end of a long day. All through my pregnancy, I just kept reminding myself of the blessing that was going to be bestowed upon me. Maybe that's why the thought of going through the final delivery suddenly seemed such an inviting proposition (as tough as that may be to believe). And then, despite the long hours I was in labour, I actually had a ball. In my head, I was breaking into disco moves. ☺

THERE IS NO SUCH THING AS BAD KIDS

Positive parenting

Parents need to fill a child's bucket of self-esteem so high that the rest of the world can't poke enough holes to drain it dry.

~ Alvin Price

When we were children, everyone tried to prepare us for the worst. Becoming a strong and independent person was a constant concern. Maybe that's why we tend to grow up thinking life is tough. But I didn't pay much heed to that and somehow, life actually hasn't been that tough for me – partially because I'm an eternal optimist and I truly believe in the power of positivity. Almost everything I have wished for has come true. *You* can achieve that too. Many people come up to me and say, "You're so confident and positive". And because my outlook on life is so deeply ingrained in my psyche, I could never understand what exactly they meant by that. Most often, I would just wonder to myself, 'Really? I am?'.

At times I felt that some people even said so with hints of negativity, but that didn't deter my zest. Then began my journey into self-help literature, and after reading many books, I discovered a connection between the compliments I received and the way I looked at life. As a child I was told I was usually confident. As a result, my confidence only grew, as did my optimism. And it was this positivity that was helping me attract all that I desired.

The magical part about this philosophy is that its effect is not limited to your life alone. It's the perfect tool to bond with your children. The imperative point here is *how*. How do we implement this tool to create an unbreakable bond with our children? How do we make them confident young adults? How do we have who are a pleasure to take into public? After all, no one wants to cringe in discomfort at dinner. Everyone wants their young ones to behave responsibly in public. How can we use this strategy to get our children to share their thoughts with us more often? And there is a simple answer to all these *how* questions – just focus on the child's positive behaviour.

Keeping a joyful and non-aggressive view will not only ensure your children know you love them, but will also encourage them to develop independent thinking much earlier in life. Children are human and have feelings just like we adults do. We all want to be spoken to with respect, right? Then why is it okay to speak to children in a negative manner? Do you want to be ordered around all the time and be told what to do at every instance? Would you like to be told that your neighbour is better at his/her job than you are?

In our life-long mission to give our children the best upbringing, we sometimes tend to forget what they really need – love. They need to be told that they are appreciated for what and how they are in that moment. We need to motivate them with positive statements. A tiny tip: *always remember that a larger issue usually triggers most of their irrational behavior.*

So next time your child does something that you consider wrong, instead of reprimanding him/her in the presence of others, just whisper to the child, "Would you like it if I did that?" or "I would never do that". You can also try asking, 'Is something bothering you?' Who doesn't like some TLC, right? The change might not be instant, but soon you will notice that your little ones will start seeing their better sides themselves. If you're persistent enough, you can even get them to have regular heart-to-hearts with you and so learn more about what's bothering them. A complete shift needs to take place. Forget firing them by saying, "Stop crying and disturbing everyone!" and concentrate more on believing and saying, "I understand you are very tired right now, and that fatigue is probably making you uncomfortable. Tell me, what do you feel like doing now?"

Positive parenting is a simple concept to implement, and the fantastic results of this will be obvious. But there is more to it. We can't discount the fact that our lives are also constantly about dealing with various sources of stress. At times it comes from comments made by fellow parents: "Is your child doing numbers yet?" or "You haven't potty trained your kid yet?". As a result of all this pressure, we sometimes tend to exhibit negativity. *Remember that nothing people say matters in the end.*

For instance, if your little ones make a mistake, instead of telling them directly that they have been naughty or bad, try giving them a hug. Tell them they do not need to feel bad about an unintentional goof-up. And then include them in the correction of their tiny slip-ups. Whenever my son drops something and seems a little embarrassed, I just hold him close to me and tell him, "Come, let's clean up the mess together". Firstly, it isn't intentional, and secondly, he feels frustrated just like you would.

All children go through those phases when you feel that they are acting up; behaving in ways you do not approve of; not listening to you; talking badly; or doing things you might find upsetting. Know that it is a phase. All children go through these. If you feel your child is picking up this particular behavior from another child or adult, create a distance between them. Also, remember that this phase will pass. The more you reiterate that your child has a good heart and is a good person, the more he/she will behave that way in the long run. By this I don't mean that you should ignore the problem. For example, if your child is being mean to other children, you must show your disapproval. At the same time, praise child by saying you know he/she is not mean and that it is good to be nice to others. If the child is copying another child's behaviour, first try to ensure they spend as little time as possible together and then have an honest conversation about the specific behavior not being copied; that it hurts others and one should never hurt the feelings of others. Though young, no age is too early for honest conversations about people, feelings, honesty, love and inculcating a sense of caring about those around us.

Issues in school also need to be discussed and dealt with using lots of compliments and positive reinforcement. Talk to your child and bring up his/her achievements. Praise them for all those times they remembered to do their homework on time. Appreciate even the smallest effort they put into cleaning the house. Let them know how great you feel when they come to give you a hug out of nowhere. When they try to do well in any sphere of life, make sure you speak highly of their intelligence. Try and squeeze in as many kind words as you can, and watch your child become more confident about his/her skills with each passing day.

It's important to avoid putting negative tags on your children at all cost. Usually these are only negative because they are based on individual perceptions (more on this in Step 6). Even if you are concerned about certain behaviors, tagging them negatively will not change that behavior but only hurt their self-esteem and confidence. So do not call your child stubborn, aggressive, naughty, mean, stupid, lazy etc. Faltering in a class full of children can't be easy on anyone; that's why you should try telling your child, "You're so good in school and in your work. You're learning something new. How cool! Would you like to study some of this at home, so I can also learn with you?"

That reminds me of a speech one of the richest men in the world, Bill Gates, made. He implied that to a great extent (and I'm paraphrasing here), that the world is a big, bad place; therefore, being tough is vital. He asked those who were listening, not to expect people to be liberal and give them chances. Let's believe for a second in what this obviously successful man had to say. If your child really is going to step out into this battlefield that is the world, shouldn't we work towards strengthening his armour with love? Shouldn't we protect them with so much self-confidence that when the world fires its worst shots, they will be able to shrug them off and walk on strong? Yes, we should. And we can!

Kind words are the music of the world. ~ F. W. Faber

Positive parenting has worked wonders for so many families around me. You start noticing a change in children's behavior within days. Nothing gives mothers and fathers more happiness and pride than watching their children react to life's most challenging decisions in a positive manner. And that uplifts the bond that you share with your kids to another level. The slight change in their expressions alone give away the fact that they are now listening attentively and understand what we are saying much better. There are a number of reasons why this works. Here are a few for you to glance over.

a. By comforting children after they have made a mistake, you help them get rid of their guilt and make them less defensive.
b. When their guard is down, the chances of them understanding and focusing on what you have to say are automatically much higher. Since they also want to prove you right and not disappoint you, they'll try harder to prove that the incident was a freak case. The more you reaffirm their goodness, the more they will want to prove it.
c. You help them develop a level of comfort with themselves, which in turn reaffirms their self-confidence. Like various books by Hay say: *You love yourself, and you will love the world*!

Here are a few instances when I used 'positive parenting'.

Nanny woes

My son had a great nanny. But she was always a bit stressed and in a hurry. As a result, my son began reflecting some of her aggressive behaviour. Though usually flawless in his conduct, while conversing with the nanny, he began losing his temper and speaking to her rudely. Instead of pulling him up directly, my husband and I asked him with a lot of love and care, "Would you want her to speak to you like that as well?". Immediately the problem surfaced crystal clear. He told us, "She keeps forcing me to eat when I really don't want to!"

Now if you, as an adult, are made to stuff yourself when you genuinely don't feel like it, how would you feel? The kid had a point. Nonetheless, we explained to him calmly that his nanny was only trying to make sure he ate well so he would grow up to become a strong young man. My son understood. He now eats his meals and makes it a point to show his empty plate to me before flexing his baby biceps.

Chocolate Sunday

Kids get pampered. That's how extended family members create a bond with children, and that's how the young ones like it. My son was two years old, and every day he would be showered with oodles of chocolates and candy from aunts, older cousins, grandparents, and friends. On one of our check-up visits, the doctor suggested we control the amount of sweets he was eating unless we wanted a cavity problem. So instead of taking away all the candy and depriving him of the joy altogether, we struck a deal (based on a fantastic piece of advice from a like-minded parent). Every Sunday he was allowed to eat all the chocolates he had collected over the week. On that day, he would make sure he brushed his teeth twice, just to be on the safe side. But none of this was a plan made by us alone. There were negotiations (children really do know how to get their way) and discussions (yes, even at two years old). I sat my baby down and explained to him that the tooth doc was afraid that if he ate too much candy, his teeth would start hurting. It was that simple. We came to this understanding in no time. On most Sundays, even when he had a stock of 20 slabs of chocolate, he would not have more than four.

But the real challenge was getting him to be honest with me about this deal. It wasn't humanly possible for me to control all the people he met. There are many people who care about him and feel buying him a bar of chocolate is a sign of affection, and it is. But how could I explain my worry to all of them? So I had a little heart-to-heart with my son and explained to him that I was really concerned about his teeth (all these chats are always reinforced with lots of love and encouraging compliments about how healthy he is). And it worked. So every time he was given a chocolate in my absence, he would come to me and say, "I was a little naughty today. I ate two chocolates, and now I feel sick!" You know why he was so honest with me? Because I continued to tell him that I believed he was a good boy with healthy habits. The more I reaffirmed this fact, the more he wanted to maintain my trust.

However, all this talk never changed the way he felt about chocolates and candy. That joy should never be taken away from a child, which is why he still loves eating them as much as he used to. He just never hides them from me. I have only been able to achieve that connection with my son because I completely avoid angry statements like, 'Why did you eat so many?', 'That's horrible!' and 'Your teeth are going to go bad!'.

Sparing the rod

During the first few months of becoming a parent, couples are, naturally and constantly, stressed. Various questions come to mind. 'Are we doing enough?' 'Why is the baby not crawling yet?' 'Is our little one showing enough progress or not?' A massive and classic worry at one stage is potty training. And not everyone can handle it well. I remember being shocked on a recent visit to my niece's school. A young boy had wet his pants and he was standing there looking to the teacher for help. When she turned around, she almost screamed at him. I was furious. Did she really think children like peeing themselves? No. Would yelling at them help them correct themselves? No, it will only scare them. Then there are those who claim that the children get lazy, and that's why they find it easier to go in their pants. Someone actually came up with this theory! How can these tiny beings that spend most of their day running around like Energizer bunnies, suddenly not have the strength to walk to the loo?

Forget expecting a schoolteacher to know how to treat a child right, a mother, who is a great friend and has been brought up with great values, also stunned me beyond belief. In a moment of such impatience, she slapped her son in front of us, when he could not make it to the bathroom in time. I was there watching this! He was three years old but that did not mean he did not feel humiliated when hit in front of others. Being treated like that by the one person whom he considers his protector, comforter, and security blanket, can cause some pretty hard-core damage, if you ask me. I'm not sure how I controlled myself that day when I was in half a mind to just explain to her what I felt, but I managed to calm down.

You must wonder how positive parenting can help with this. Well, it can! I started potty training my son when he was six months old (yes, I started early). Every time I knew he wanted to go *poo poo*, I would quickly place him on the baby potty, and in no time he got acquainted with the fact that the potty was connected with him going. So there was never any waiting for him to pass stool. He would automatically do the job and we'd be back to cuddling. I also feel I got a bit lucky (refer to: Think It. Get It! for this process).

I read a lot about children before becoming a mother, so I knew that this process cannot be hastened and that all children move out of diapers naturally when the time is right. So I chose not to push him at all. Every time he sat on the potty for number one or number two, I would just smile at him and tell him how much I loved him. "I am so proud of you! You are becoming such a big boy!" would be my stance on the matter. I remember an odd year after we stopped using diapers, when my son one day did *pee pee* in his pants in the rain. Then he did that again a day later. I thought about what the problem was and realized that I needed to ask him to use the bathroom more often during the rains. I could have got upset with him or just laughed – which he undoubtedly would have noticed, but I would have only caused damage by doing either. So I shared the blame with him by apologizing and saying, "I'm sorry I did not ask you if you wanted to go to the loo earlier". Hugs always follow these statements. By sharing part of the responsibility, he felt he had company in the sticky spot he was in. Therefore, it became easier for him to understand how to avoid the situation in the future. So I reduced the humiliation and ensured his self-confidence was intact. Since then, it has never happened again.

While I have propagated positive parenting extensively in the last few pages, I also understand that we parents are but human. It might be most important to always maintain a smiling and patient *avatar* in front of the little, impressionable ones, but at the same time, on certain bad days it is possible for us to get worried and irritated with the children. And there is no reason one should be ashamed of that. It is normal. Don't feel guilty for having a bad day; everyone is allowed a few. Yes, parenting is tough! But then that's the beauty of the challenge too. Many young couples spend the first few years of their married lives just taking care of a gazillion things and forgetting themselves altogether. We run our homes, manage our jobs, and take care of our children, school, classes, food, vitamins, and so on. All this, put together, can get exhausting and make us irritable. Ask yourself: 'How often do I get angry with my children?'. This question is only for some self-introspection, so no one else needs to know.

Remember, all parents (and children too, actually), are permitted to have a few bad days! When that happens to you, instead of bottling it up inside, deal with it openly –go to your room and scream your lungs out, step into the bathroom and cry till you feel light again, or just sit in a corner and focus on your breathing for a few minutes. Whatever works! Watching a good film may do it for many. Sometimes it is even okay to share your day with your infant. Why not? Tell your child, "Mommy is a bit sad or stressed today". You will notice suddenly that your child, who you were taking care of all this while, will emerge as an unbeatable support system. Normally I get a hug from my son when I tell him I'm not having the best day, and then he cracks a joke or two and has me in splits before I know it. Trust me, shrinks aren't capable of such fast and effective results.

If you channel your frustrations better and handle situations that are usually considered tricky, with a lot more positivity and openness, you will start noticing a remarkable change in your relationship with your children. Instead of worrying, positive talk is the way into your baby's life. Tell your child that he/she is strong, loving, intelligent, gentle, caring, compassionate, talented and the most beautiful present life has give you… and it will all come true – leaving you feeling happier and more satisfied with the magical relationship you share.

Be Happy Tips

1. Stay away from being negative and negatively tagging your child at any time.
2. Practice positive affirmations as often as possible.
3. Compliment your child for little achievements and efforts.
4. Handle tricky and angry situations with positivity and patience.
5. Hitting your child will only make you and the child unhappy; there are better ways to get your point across.
6. If there are negative remarks from school or outsiders, handle them with tact and positivity so that your child's self-confidence remains intact.

YES YOU CAN!

Use positive negotiation

The way you speak to another is most likely the same way you will be spoken to. ~ Unknown

Much of what I have to say here is an extension of the

previous segment on positive parenting. But because the significance of this is so vital, I thought it deserved a section devoted to it. In the next few pages, I've focused on the importance of saying *yes* a lot more and uttering *no* a lot less, when talking to your children. Many of us took the conscious decision to become parents, while others just realized one fine morning that they'd have a baby running around the house in a matter of nine months. Either way, if you have children or you're on your way to becoming a parent, congratulations! There is truly nothing as satisfying as watching your baby grow into a beautiful adult. But before that happens, you invest many years in the upbringing of children. They are young, impressionable, and a big responsibility. Often, you understand their needs and wants a lot better than they do themselves. But never does that mean that they don't have rights of their own!

These privileges may not be written on paper, but children have the right to freedom, to making choices and being their own bosses. You might have given birth to them, but they are their own decision-makers. There are two golden rules to follow at this stage: *you are not the boss* and *your child is always right*.

A thousand contradictory thoughts must be running through your mind: 'Of course, we know better when it comes to what the child needs', 'We want the best for them', 'We are more experienced', 'They are too young to tell good from bad', and so on. I completely understand. All these thoughts come from love and care. So trust me when I say that all I intend to presenting here is a new perspective. Let's begin by asking ourselves a few questions. What makes us feel we are more equipped to take certain decisions for them? Is it the fact that we have had more experiences in life? Okay. But isn't experience a sum total of what we learn from our past failures? So why are we restricting our children's thoughts to our failures? Aren't we killing their spirit and creativity by limiting their freedom based on our past? One word, if ignored, can change the life of a child – *no*. How often do we end up saying *no* to our children?

"May I eat chocolate?"……"No!"
"May I paint the wall red?"……"No!"
"May I go out and play (when it's time for bed)?"….."No!"
"May I stick my finger in the electric plug point?"….."No!"
"May I become a rock star?"….."No!"

Usually, in the larger scheme of things, these are irrelevant. What do we achieve? Yes, there are moments when you don't know where to begin explaining to children what greasy and oily food can do to their gentle systems. Half the time they don't listen. The other half is spent dealing with tantrums and pretty much each time we are killing their spirit and dampening their creativity in minute doses.

Instead, to begin with, take a few minutes in a day and just go with the flow. Say *yes* to every bizarre, and at times unachievable, demand. Let the child believe that anything is possible! And in order to make that happen, throw the word *no* out of your vocabulary when you're dealing with your baby. For instance, if your little one insists on eating a burger from a junk-food joint, you can present to them the option of a nice, yummy and healthier one that you will make especially for him/her. Though if you go by what I have suggested in the chapter about the vegetable war, this situation might never present its messy face.

When children are first introduced to color pencils and crayons, they tend to use the entire house as their canvas. The next time your child asks you whether he/she can paint the walls red, you can say something like, "Of course you can. Just give me five minutes to put up this lovely white chart paper on the wall, which will make the colours look even brighter!" And if your child expresses the desire to pursue a far-fetched and bizarre career, definitely do not say no. Crushing dreams at such a tender age will not do anyone any good in the long run.

The idea is not to make unrealistic claims. Children can come up with crazy questions, answers to which you will not have imagined in your wildest dreams! Instead of nipping the query in the bud, encourage conversation. Bring the talk to a logical conclusion and they themselves will understand your point. This way, not only are you giving them the confidence to believe that they have deduced the meaning on their own, but also the faith that you, as a parent, will not unnecessarily deny them anything.

Like you have ways of dealing with your own boss at work, there are tricks that you can try your hand at while managing your child's demands as well. The three most-workable ones are:

1. Postpone
2. Distract
3. Negotiate

Here is how I used the three marvellous techniques.

1. Postpone: Remember the distorted saying, *Why do something today, if you can do it tomorrow*? Well, I'm not asking you to do any such thing. However, when your child wants to visit a friend's house at an inappropriate time, this saying does comes in handy. Sort of. Instead of responding with, "No, you can't," say "Of course, you can go. I will call his/her mom right now and ask her if we can come over tomorrow! Then she'll have time to prepare the cookie mixture for you to make nice chocolate chip biscuits."
2. Distract: If that technique doesn't work, bring out an option. Nothing like being distracted by something so exciting that everything else seems boring. Try using the movie card: "Hey, do you want to watch a super fun film?"or "How about a nice drive?" Often, when the moment has passed, children tend to forget what minutes ago they were dying to do! Mission accomplished.
3. Negotiate: Strike a deal. Say "Okay, you can meet your friend in the park. But only if you promise to leave in an hour without creating a fuss". Negotiate with children like you would with adults. It actually works wonders. In those rare cases when neither of the first two methods comes in handy, you have to let your negotiating skills shine.

I agree that saying *yes* to and for everything might not be easy. It requires lots of patience and time. But in the end, you will realize that both you and your child will feel better. In some situations you will not have to entirely give children what they want if you reach the negotiation stage. If my four-year-old, for instance, was to tell me that he wanted to drive the car, this is how I would manage the situation despite saying *yes*.

- ✓ "Of course you can. As soon as it's parked in a safe place (and the keys are in my bag), you can take charge of the wheel."
- ✓ If that doesn't work and he says, "Mom, I don't want to drive with the car turned off, I want to control the wheel when the engine is on!", then I would say, "Okay, how about I buy you that super cool Ferrari replica that you can drive around with an awesome wireless remote? That will be a present just because you're so special!" By letting the child know that driving a remote-controlled miniature is a lot more fun (which it sometimes truly is), you're making sure your child knows that he/she is getting the better deal out of the bargain.
- ✓ If the demand still persists, then I would say, "You can drive the car, but as soon as you are 18 years old. And look at you, you're nearly there! See how fast your muscles are growing."

Communicating and spending time listening to what your child has to say (Step 3: Don't Just Hear, Listen), will make sure your thoughts are attuned with your child's. As a result, when it comes to negotiating and distracting the little one, you will know exactly what will work. Within no time, saying *yes* more, will become second nature.

Another quick technique that works is simple questioning. If your son/daughter is feeling cranky on a Saturday evening and suddenly says something like, "Mom/Dad, I want to come with you for your night out," then try and put the child in your position by posing a few questions. Ask the child whether he/she would like you to go along to all their sleepovers and game sessions. Would they like their parents to throw a tantrum when they are going out to play? Chances are children will develop objectivity about their behavior and send you off to your party with a big smile.

Now, most parents also go through the toys issue, when children have too many toys and still want more. So we worry about retaining their values in a world of excess. Firstly, honestly, kids initially love toys made with kitchen utensils or simple things you find anyway at home. But all parents and friends want to pamper their child with gifts, or sometimes with weekends where you just go to a toy store and keep buying toys. Seriously, realize that these toys are made to be as appealing to parents as to children; the big toy companies know who finally makes a product a success (being attractive to parent as much as to children). So while we continue the 'saying yes' rule, we do a few things to balance this. Maybe have a rule that the child gives a toy away for every one you buy. Expose him/her to the less privileged, and to be thankful for the things they already have instead of wanting even more. Children will value what they get and learn to give and share, from your example of contentment. As long as we communicate the values we believe in and practice them ourselves, children will pick up the good habits as well.

You can try these tricks I have shared with you, but there are a few pointers to keep in mind. First and foremost, never force your child to do anything. If you succeed in maintaining this one rule, none of your strategies will fail. Remember the child is always right. The child's behavior might reflect something else, but it comes from the intrinsic mechanism nature has blessed him/her with.

A few months ago, a colleague was complaining to me how her daughter refused to have her mug of milk in the morning. She had been struggling with this matter for weeks and was trying very hard not to resort to force. I suggested she speak to her daughter about why she would not. Later that night, when she spoke to her five-year-old, she told her mom that she had been having some irritation in the throat, and that's why she did not feel like having the milk. We all know that mother nature knows best. The little girl didn't know why she didn't feel like having milk at the onset of a slight congestion, but her system did. That's why she was refusing.

Trust your children's instincts, which are strong and not oppressed like ours are. You'll be surprised to see how aware they are of their bodies and minds. Sometimes I feel it is the adults who need to unlearn and relearn some basics. I'm actually married to one example of this don't-force-your-child/say-yes-more theory's effectiveness. My in-laws were liberal in their thinking when my husband was a little boy. Instead of holding him back from unscrewing and pulling apart all his cars, mechanics, toys, and even door knobs at times, they would encourage him. Some of his aunts and uncles called him 'destructive', but his parents felt he was 'curious'.

Even when they look back now, they say, "He used to operate on the cars because he wanted to become an engineer". And that's exactly what he became. He enjoys innovation and creative concepts and testing new machinery, and waking up every Monday and going to office to do just that. His love for his job has remained innocent and untouched over the years. Probably, if had been told as a child to 'stop being destructive', he would not have the same passion for his profession that he does today.

In the end, if all the strategies you applied have refused to work in your favor, and your child is still adamant to have what he/she wants, then you have to oblige. If you have not been able to change the child's mind, then be ready to 'stand by your word'. By doing that and keeping your promises, children tend to feel respected. They will happily understand your point of view thereafter, and you can 'agree to disagree' peacefully, if that's what it comes to. They will never take you for granted or ever mistrust a claim you have made. If you reciprocate with the same maturity and respect, they too, will want to stand by the promises they have made, which is undeniably a valuable life lesson.

Honesty and keeping your promises are both very important. Keep your promises and children will keep theirs. Of course, we are human and it is not always possible to stay conscious of our conduct. But, as long as we try and correct ourselves when we falter, I believe we are being good parents. Maintain your parenting philosophy and you will see amazing results.

Human beings are all creatures of habit. Therefore, it is crucial for children to be regularly exposed to behavior you want them to endorse. And the one way you can do that is by remaining consistent in your own mannerisms and reactions. Consistency is essential during these stages. About a year ago, my son developed a cavity. My husband and I were worried and the worry drove us to force him to brush better. Force was against our own basic parenting approach. So, after getting the cavity filled, we insisted that he brush his teeth properly and for longer than usual. Our fears were driving that insistence. Initially he resisted and even cried. Then we realized what we were doing – we apologized for forcing him and explained the situation in detail. Directly and indirectly, we communicated the importance of brushing correctly. And in a matter of months, the morning process that used to be a crying fiesta, magically became part of his daily routine. It works, Eureka!

Be Happy Tips

1. Never force your child. Don't hold him/her down, drag, trick, or use fear as a means to get the job done. None of these are good in the long term.
2. Say *yes* more often! Avoid saying *no* at all costs. It dampens your child's creativity and confidence levels. Anyway, it's an overrated and negative word. You can do without it.
3. Your child is a human being and deserves the same right to make an informed decision as you do. Give him/her the freedom to do that.
4. While dealing with a child, try to use methods of negotiation

or distraction, or attempt to postpone the event. Talk to your child to convince him/ her of your concerns. Let the child decide.

5. Though unlikely, if you still have not succeeded despite implementing all the above-mentioned strategies, then be ready to give in to the child's demands. Playing fair is important, after all!
6. Consistency in your parenting philosophy is important.
7. Be honest with your child and keep your promises, and the child will do the same in return.

INVISIBLE INSPIRATION

Strengthening the subconscious

Whatever we plant in our subconscious mind and nourish with repetition and emotion will one day become a reality.

~ Earl Nightingale

The unlimited power of the subconscious isn't a new concept to humanity. Till now, I've spoken of tapping into the resources of that hidden section of our minds to find happiness. In this chapter, I will show you how you can use the same for the betterment of your little ones' lives. I have discussed how envisioning positive thoughts can change your world. It drives away negativity and helps you to achieve and attract your dreams. Now you can use the same power to create magical moments with your children. Of course, there is always the effective method of reinforcing your children's self-images by persistently being positive and encouraging them in all their endeavors. But there are also a few, techniques you can implement to implant healthy and beautiful thoughts in their minds without actually having to sit them down.

Sleep counselling

This method follows the same principle as a lullaby. Just as a relaxing voice can put a hyperactive child to sleep happily, certain thoughts, when conveyed to children in their sleep, take effect without you even realizing it. While your child is in dreamland, his/her subconscious mind is quietly at work, listening. If you feel your child hasn't been eating his greens very well, or you've noticed that he/she has been combating a blocked nose very often, try this: ten minutes after put him/her to sleep, gently whisper positive affirmations into their ear. Convey strengthening and positive statements to the child's system. Say things like: '(Child's name) is a healthy boy/girl' or '(Child's name) is growing well and feels healthy and strong'. Softly send loads of affirmative energy to their subconscious. But make sure that you don't use any negative words in the process. Avoid saying, for instance: 'You *don't* have a cold,' or 'You will *not* eat unhealthy food'.

Even the slightest hint of negativity can hinder the process and send out confused messages. Be clear and simple in your speech, and if you feel singing to them will help, then by all means serenade them into improving their lives. By contacting their subliminal selves directly, you are not only helping them develop a better understanding of various concepts but also comforting their nerves.

I am a firm believer in this technique because it worked on me, and I was 24 not 4! When I got married, for many nights my husband spoke to me about the joyful experience that parenting really is. I hadn't thought about having a baby back then. My husband, meanwhile, was older and super excited about starting a family. So every night, while I lay there asleep, he whispered these affirmative thoughts into my ear, literally! In a matter of three months, I found myself feeling increasingly upbeat about becoming a mom. Then one fine morning, I woke up and knew I wanted to experience the magical journey of parenthood. I still haven't stopped thanking him, to be honest. And I don't think I will ever do so either!

When my son was much younger, he would resist having baths and changing clothes. He was two months old at that point. And at the risk of sounding a bit loony, let me tell you that I would talk to him regularly. I helped him calm down by playing soothing music during our deep-in-sleep chatting sessions and told him how good staying clean feels. I recall a friend facing a peculiar problem. She would often be told things like, 'Your son is so tiny,' sometimes even in the presence of her child. She feared that the child's young soul must have been hurt. But I explained to her that nothing people say is important. I suggested that every night, when her son was asleep, she should reaffirm the fact that he was a strong boy and growing well. In moments when he felt insecure and would refuse to let her leave the house, I insisted she remind him of what an independent, confident, and mature boy he was. And we did indeed watch his behavior change in a positive manner.

It is equally, if not more, important to also keep reminding your children that you are always there for them, no matter what. Once they know that, even their subconscious will be more receptive to your messages.

The silent listener

We all know that children have sharp ears. Especially when it comes to overhearing conversations where they've heard their names mentioned, their senses are automatically heightened. But instead of worrying about what they may get exposed to as a result of this curiosity, know that you can use this trait to help them feel great about themselves. Talk positively and appreciatively about your child in front of your friends, when the little ones can actually hear you. It will make them want to stand up to the responsibilities they unknowingly have been entrusted with. Not only will they feel like they've been given a shot of self-esteem in the arm, but they will also appreciate the fact that you, as a parent, think so highly of them.

Secondary messages have a massive impact on a child's psyche. What children hear, when you feel they aren't really listening, can have a long-lasting effect on their minds. Filtering all this information would obviously be a mammoth task, so don't worry. If you realize you've said something wrong in the presence of your child, don't hesitate to apologize instantly.

It's perfectly okay to make a mistake; we'reall human. If children hear you having a fight, discuss the matter openly with them and tell them what made mom or dad so angry. Confess! Open your heart to them, and they will follow suit. It's always better just to talk things out. If you have certain behavioural patterns that you yourself are not too proud of, then don't hide them or lie about them. Make the children part of your self-improvement process. Like them, you too, are growing with each passing day and learning new things. Let them know that their parents also are human and can err, and that it is absolutely okay to accept one's shortcomings.

Over the years, this unconstrained flow of communication will lead to a lot of mutual respect. Your child is a reflection of who you are. Remember, even when you think children are not listening, they are. When you feel they don't know the truth, they do.

Be Happy Tips

1. The power of the subconscious mind is untapped and immense. Harness it and address your concerns magically. For instance, if your child has a congested nose, ten minutes after the child is asleep, whisper positive words into his/her ear. Tell the child that he/she is healthy and fit.
2. Your children may be busy playing with their toys, but remember that they have super sharp ears. They are always listening. Talk positively about them especially when they are around. They like hearing

what you have to say about them to your friends and family members.

3. Don't be afraid to apologize. If you feel something you have done has hurt your child's sentiments, say sorry. Explain why you behaved in a manner you are not proud of, and the child will understand and become your support system. Of course, make sure loads of hugs follow during and after!

STEP 3

BE THE PERSON YOU WANT YOUR CHILD TO BE

Communication, Respect, Health and more…

DON'T JUST HEAR, LISTEN

Real Communication

Good, the more communicated, more abundant grows.

~ John Milton

Good communication skills help us achieve so much in life. And when that talent is combined with the innate understanding of a parent regarding his/her child, it can work magic. Look beyond the screams and tears, and listen to what your child is truly trying to say. It is true that you know more about life than your few-years-old child does, but that does not mean you don't have to concentrate on every sign of communication your child exhibits. I know children scream sometimes; they also get cranky and just talk in *goo goo ga ga* language at times. But no matter what, always make sure you listen patiently to what your child is trying to tell you. I do. Parents best understand the expressions and feelings of their children. They instinctively know what is making their child irritable long before a doctor is consulted. But children obviously aren't as fluent in any language as you, so they try to use other ways of communicating with us.

Each time you see your children exhibit any peculiar behavior, try and empathize with them, and hear them out. You may just realize there is a valid reason why they are acting in a certain manner. For instance, if your baby does not like drinking milk or eating green, leafy vegetables, instead of trying to force or trick him/her into eating them, talk to them positively and make them understand why they should. Make dealing with difficult foods a fun game or a joyful competition. Tell them eating right will help them get better at a sport such as football (and that's true; a stronger body tires less on the field).

You know what will work best for your child and what won't, so sell the concept. But do it positively. I know I did, and it still works wonders. Rather than using my authoritative voice, I just go in with a smile on my face and with an open mind (always be ready for negotiations when dealing with the little masters). And trust me, once you achieve what you wanted all along, nothing feels as good as watching your children smile. Children also have their own thoughts, feelings, opinions and preferences, and if we patiently hear them out, not only do they feel respected but they will want to hear us out aswell when we are communicating with them. Inculcate a relationship where communication is the key, both ways, and you will see the benefits for yourself. there are some children who are innately good communicators while others are not and hesitate to share. But if you do your best, communicate your thoughts, feelings etc. in a loving, respectful way, in time they will also reflect the same behavior.

Here are some examples of times when I have succeeded in communicating with my son in tough situations and beyond.

Give them time to open up

A few months ago, I was scheduled to take my son to the eye doctor for a general check-up. While we drove to the clinic, he remained unusually silent and spent most of his time staring out of the window. He trusted me, so he knew what I was asking of him was important, but I could sense some anxiety. When we got to the doctor's office, my son threw a fit. He refused to budge, cried his heart out, and just did not want to enter the doctor's room. I knew something was wrong because he normally never reacted in this way. He had been scared of doctors when he was younger but he had outgrown that fear years ago. So, after trying to convince him a few times, I gave him a few minutes to gather himself and calm down. I didn't force him to enter the doctor's chamber nor did I threaten him in any manner. The doctor, who had been waiting all that while, understood the situation. Then, slowly I tried starting a conversation about what was troubling him. In moments when a child is stressed and is not old enough to communicate fluently, parents must give them time. Once they know they aren't under any pressure, slowly and steadily they naturally reveal their thoughts.

I asked him why he was so worried, because I had told him earlier that all that the doctor wanted to do was show him some colorful pictures and talk to him. After about ten minutes, he came up to me and confessed why he was petrified. "Mama, the doctor is going to give me an injection in my eye," he said to me in whispered tones. My heart nearly stopped for a second. I am still scared of getting a needle prick in my bum; I could not even imagine the kind of terror my baby was living in. Just the thought of injections is horrible, even for adults.

If we hadn't bothered giving him the time to open up, imagine how much damage that fear would have caused. In his heart, he would have thought, 'My parents are forcing me to get an injection in my eye'. I gave him a big hug and explained that there was no injection; his eye would not hurt at the end of the session, and that I would never let him go through anything like that. I shared with him the thought that what was worrying him would also have scared his mommy!

Having heard everything I had to say, he said, "Okay, let me think about this" (yes, he actually talks like that sometimes). Within ten minutes he had wiped away his tears, smiled at me, and said, "Okay, I'm bored of sitting here". He grabbed my little finger and led me into the clinic. He did well at the tests and paid attention and in the end the doctor told us there were no issues with the boy's eyesight. Had I forced him into that room, he would have been scared, could have botched up the tests, and had a little less trust in me. None of which I was willing to take a chance on. Now, in moments like these, it's easy to give into pressure – you're situated in a public place, the doctor has been kept waiting, and a bit of a scene is being created in front of outsiders. But all that isn't important. Your bond with your child is. Giving matters like these a little time proves that these issues can be resolved calmly.

We create their fears

Everyone knows children are generally afraid of the dark. The uncertainty of what lies between the child and that lampshade button can be quite terrifying. Maybe that's why quite a few adults who are scared of the dark too. But somehow these childish fears aren't taken seriously. When the little ones think twice before entering a dark room or alley, some parents just ignore their hesitation and egg them on. I've personally seen folks try and motivate their children to get over their fears by saying things like, 'C'mon, don't be a sissy,' and 'There's nothing there', and trying to get the child to 'man' up.

Where do you think these fears come from? How many times have you seen or heard parents use the words 'monster', 'doctor', or 'police' as devices to convince children to eat their food, sleep on time, not walk out of the house at night, or refrain from talking to strangers? Quite a few, if I'm not wrong. Even though most parents use these techniques for the safety of the child, they may not realize that the damage caused can be deep. It is not a positive tactic to use to get your child to listen. You can't get him/her to 'listen' by using irrational fears, but you can get the child's attention by explaining things logically. Don't try to scare your child into submission, because those hidden fears can become mental blocks over time and surface at later stages of life.

However, uncontrolled media exposure is also another reason such thoughts enter children's minds. TV shows, cartoons, comic books, graphic novels, daily news, superheroes, films, and so on... in some way or the other, depict violence, scary monsters, and dangerous situations. We obviously can't be expected to start filtering each and every thing children watch and read. That would get a bit constraining for children too. I know I would hate it. But what we can do is to be around to talk about their fears. Ask them what they think of certain shows, or just have a conversation about the dreaded topic. When my son told me he was afraid of walking into the bedroom when the lights were turned off, instead of pushing him, I sat him down and spoke to him about what he was thinking and feeling. He told me he was scared because "there could be monsters" hiding behind the door. So I explained that there were no such things as monsters. Those creatures were just figments of people's imaginations and were meant to entertain people, not scare them. But convincing him wasn't that easy. The TV had also reaffirmed what he had seen in those comics. "I saw the monsters on that show I watched," he told me. That reminded me of when I was a child myself, every time a particular song would air on TV, I'd scurry behind the set to see if tiny people were dancing around behind the screen (yes, everyone has an imagination; mine was a little hyperactive, I guess).

At this point, I knew I could use this situation not only to nullify his fears, but also to introduce my son to the concept of television. So after explaining the truth behind the tube to him in theory, I asked him to draw a flower. Then I held up the drawing to him and asked him whether he believed what he had made was a real flower? "No," he said. "Just like this drawing, what you see on cartoon shows on TV have been made by someone and are not real," I told him. He immediately understood. Suddenly, stepping into that dark room was not such a big obstacle. Even though I was there holding his hand tight for the first few times, I knew he would get used to it in no time.

Parent-child chats

This point is really close to my heart. Whether it is about small daily issues or general banter, I love talking to my son. I share my happiness with him, just like I tell him about my bad days. That's one reason why, despite him not being a natural communicator, he still communicates with me as freely as he does. Now is the perfect time to inculcate these skills. I know many people have trouble talking about their issues or even opening up in front of their closest associates. All this is usually the deep-rooted effect of not having communicated as a child. Give children the same patient hearing that you would give to a friend who is going through a difficult time or a break-up. Talk to your children like they are equals and your friends. Give them a chance to form their own opinions; spend time with them and be attentive when they are speaking. What goes around does come around. If you respect what your baby has to say, he/she will reciprocate.

For the first few years, children take a lot of time to become coherent in their communication. They are growing at the speed of light, and every day they observe and learn a thousand new things, words, textures, expressions, feelings, tastes, fears, reactions, and so on. I know I'd fumble in my speech if I had that much going on in my mind all the time. So be patient and forgiving. Ignore those little repetitions and speech errors and focus on enjoying these moments. If they ask you the same question twice or even thrice, be patient. Talk to them like you would wish to be spoken to, and you'll notice the effectiveness of this technique. Sometimes they may not know how to express their concerns clearly, so cross-question them, give them options they can choose from, describe similar instances they can use as references to explain themselves, and don't give up! But do all this with love – hold hands, smile, and let them know that you are only there to help them feel better. And I assure you, they will put down their guards and feel no fear of judgment.

Usually, if you respond to a question with aggression, you will notice that the next time the child has something he/she wants to ask you, he/she will end up thinking twice. You obviously do not want this to happen. You might think being a child is a joyride, but even children have stresses and issues they deal with. From being bullied at school to losing best friends, things can get pretty bad. If your child shares a comfortable relationship with you, he/she can come and pour his/her heart out. The child can tell you about all his/her worries and fears, and so lighten the load on the mind, which is very helpful.

I remember my son once came to me looking forlorn. He said, "I don't know why Vidhu (a good friend), doesn't play with me anymore. He even tried to hit me the other day." How can you not want to hug the little soul in moments like these? So I held him close to me and shared with him a life lesson which probably no one his age would have ever heard: "We can't control how others react. As long as you are good to people, you will always have friends."

Communication is a highly underrated aspect of human relationships. I personally have a very open relationship with my parents. I speak to them regularly, and make sure I share my innermost feelings with them. They also feel loved and trusted by my behavior. It is believed that children who don't communicate when they are young, are more likely to fall prey to addictions and weaknesses, as they don't have a support system they can rely upon. Despite my parents' stellar advice, I did mess up sometimes, but even then, as a teenager, they did not condemn me. And because they didn't judge me for sharing my adventures with them, I did not feel the need to rebel. So every time they had something to say to me, I knew they meant it for the best, because I trusted them with all my heart. Unlike many species, humans have been blessed with a heightened sense of communication. But we don't always manage to utilize that benefit as we should.

I went through phases that any youngster does. I wanted to experiment and go out partying and have a wild time too. My parents never stopped me from doing anything. They never said no. The only piece of advice they gave to me was, "Do what you must, but please make sure you are with us or in the company of people who truly love you. And always be prepared to say no to something you are uncomfortable doing." I could live with that! That rule made life so much easier for my entire family and me. I never tried any vices alone, but because I felt the need to experience certain things (who doesn't right?), I made sure my parents were always in the loop.

I know that if I follow a similar path when it comes to bringing up my child, I will not be disappointed. Rather than finding out from school, his friends, or worse, my nosey neighbors, I would rather have *my* son tell me that he wants to go get a drink (when he's old enough). I want to be part of his youth as a friend and confidanté, and the forging of that bond begins in infancy. All we have to do is not fall into the trap of societal and peer pressures, and automatically our minds will remain free. Why should we limit our beliefs to what is publicly considered right or wrong? Why can't we be the judges of our own actions and form our own opinions?

If your children want to be experimental in life, let them. Remember, they will find a way to do so, with or without your knowledge. The difference is that when you are aware of what they are up to, you will stress less, and they will not want to disappoint you by being reckless. If we really want to protect and not control our children, we must give them the option to fall and learn. Let them choose their experiences, but be there if they falter.

Now all this serious talk aside, communication isn't just about 'issues'. Just taking five or ten minutes from your day to catch up with your child is equally important. Just sit and chat. Before my son goes to bed at night, he makes it a point to come over and say to me, "Mom, let's talk!" I know there will be people (I can think of a few right now, and I'm sure you can too), who will make fun of you for doing this. They'll probably say, "C'mon, don't make your son into a sissy!" But I don't care what they think. I know my son will grow up to be an incredibly smart, communicative, and mature adult. All those people who feel a strong man has to put up that tough, I-don't-need-to-talk-about-my-issues exterior, well...

all I can say is that they don't know what they are missing out on. Being able to communicate is a gift. Let's use it to create a beautiful bond of love, trust, and security. Moms and dads, I promise you will love every minute of it.

Be Happy Tips

1. You have the gift of intrinsically understanding your child; enjoy this, but also focus on verbal communication with him/her.
2. Be patient and give children the extra time they need to express what they need and don't try to instantly correct them.
3. Talk to your child when you think something is troubling him/her or when you are concerned about something.
5. Set some time aside every day for parent-child chats, as this is time wonderfully spent.

BELIEVE IT OR NOT YOUR BABY IS HUMAN!

Children deserve respect

A person's a person, no matter how small. ~ Dr. Seuss

How would you feel if someone held your head down and began pouring water on it? Not very nice. Though the aim might be to wash your hair and keep it clean, wouldn't you have liked to be told about it in advance? Or maybe asked? Children are young and have not learnt the ropes of life, but that does not mean they cannot be treated with dignity. Treat your children as you would your partner, parents, grandparents, or even a friend. They deserve it! You will notice that your children will start reciprocating that behaviour. There are three vital truths you should keep in mind in this context.

- Kids have feelings just like adults.
- Don't force decisions on them. Inform them first, then have a conversation, and you won't face any opposition.
- Be sensitive to their public image. No one likes being humiliated, especially in front of others.
- Respect them and expect the same respect back from them.

The more you treat a child like an infant, the harder he/she will try to get you to take them seriously. Why should a little baby be expected to do any such thing? Many believe that once people have children their social lives come to a standstill... at least for a few years. But that is the result of a choice that people make. It doesn't have to be so. My husband and I understand how important it is to sometimes step out of the parenthood zone and unwind. And before every weekend, we make sure we have a conversation with our son about our plans first. He respects our decisions, and we respect his. The key point here is that children need to be informed, and if they demand an explanation/cancellation, then it can be discussed and talked through. They need to know why going out is important for you, and once they understand that, they will happily kiss you goodbye for the evening.

You should never disappear. How would you like being left alone at home while your family members are out partying without even a 'bye? Or would you like walking out into the living room only to see that the two people who are your protectors have quietly slipped out? We, as parents, need to give children a lot of respect. Have discussions with them like you would with anyone your age. You will realize they will start trusting you more and feel increasingly confident about themselves.

When dealing with children on a day-to-day basis, try not to order them around. Whether it is to pick up their toys or tidy their rooms, request them instead. You could say, "Wouldn't it be nice if everyone could contribute, in their own small way, to keeping the house neat?". The next time you are dusting the shelves on your own, you may notice some help coming your way. You may have noticed that children usually do take a lot of initiative to keep their surroundings clean. In moments like those, we get worried about them picking up infections when they are surrounded by germs and dust. As a result, we stop them from doing so. Then a few years later we begin asking them to help around again. The signals we're giving out tend to get a bit confusing, don't they? Let's try not to allow that to happen.

Sometimes children tend to get rebellious or just defiant. Everyone has phases! If they've said something hurtful, try not to react. Instead, ask them later whether they would like to be treated in the same manner. You'll be stunned to see how sensitive children really are. Like I said earlier, children are the reflections of their parents. If we empathize with them, they do the same. And if we ignore them, they react in a similar manner.

You will notice that there are a few instances in this book that mention my son and his nanny, who incidentally is much older than I. Since she belongs to an older generation and school of upbringing, her techniques of dealing with my son were very different from ours. She believed that 'children are very young, and they don't understand anything'. My husband and I, on the other hand, follow a philosophy that's exactly the opposite. As a result, when our son would communicate with her on the basis of what we had taught him, there would always be some conflict, following which, he would get upset. I dealt with this problem by explaining to the nanny what was going wrong. Consistency in parenting methods plays a very important role in shaping your child's personality and future. Therefore, all primary caretakers should also follow the same guidelines. If your child needs a shower and doesn't necessarily love jumping into one, instead of forcing the child, talk and prepare the child for the hair wash that's coming. Let the child smell the fragrance of the shampoo and make him/her understand that you are only helping them stay clean. For all you know, there may be a reason your child does not like having their hair washed. If you have an open discussion about it, those fears may surface and you will be able to deal with them.

This strategy of talking to your child about their day's schedule, can be implemented right from the start. Yes, even before they can talk! When our son was a few months old, he didn't enjoy being bathed. So, minutes before it was time for him to be given a bath, I would start talking to him about the process as I undressed him step by step. I would explain the entire plan to him as he looked at me wide-eyed. I would say, "I am taking you to the bathroom now, then I am going to place you on the bath seat. Now, I'm going to pour a little water on your tummy…" and so on. You may think the child doesn't understand our language, but the communication between a child and a parent goes way beyond words. Once you carry out the action, after you've explained it to the child, they do not get taken by surprise and immediately fathom what you were trying to tell them. I wanted to try this technique, which I learnt at a parenting course, to test its workability. And it proved itself!

In the daily routine of our lives, we might not realize sometimes that so many small tantrums can be avoided just by treating children with respect like adults. There are always some tasks that are tougher than others to deal with, but there is a way for everything. For instance, when parents are trying to convince their children to take their medicines, they tend to use some harmless tricks to do the job. But how would you like to be fooled into believing that you're going to take a sip of honey, when the actual cough syrup probably tastes completely different? Why should they be subjected to such trickery? Explain to your child that the medicine will make him feel healthy and super strong. Children understand logic a lot better than we do with our biased minds. Let them know it's a matter of a few days, after which they will feel as fit as a fiddle.

The above-mentioned instance also addresses the subject of honesty, which is directly related to respect. Don't we all respect honest people? Well, if you want your child to be frank with you at all times, then you need to set an example by being extremely open and honest with him/her. Don't throw up any unpleasant surprises. Tell children what they can expect for dinner and what weekend events they can look forward to. And if you make a mistake, make sure you accept it and apologize.

Embarrassment is another sentiment that most adults are very self-conscious about. Yet, when it comes to children, we don't expect them to feel embarrassed. This is a myth. Why can they not feel ashamed? Like us, they too, want to develop a good public image and enjoy being appreciated and the center of attention. No one wants to be spoken to negatively, and at that young and impressionable age, one embarrassing moment can do more harm than imagined. So treat them well, look past their tiny mistakes in public places, like you would ignore or cover up an adult's *faux pas*. It is extremely important for you to remain consistent in your efforts. Only if you continue to react to certain stimulus in the same manner over a considerable period of time, will they understand your effort. It really is as simple as that. Be gentle and kind when it comes to dealing with children, especially before outsiders. Even when you're appreciating someone else's child in front of your own, never compare the two. Let your children feel they will always stand apart for you. Eventually, you'll realize that this behavior has two magical advantages – not only does it make children happier, but it also urges them to act appropriately in public. On top of that, they will also respect you, your values, your thoughts, and all that you have to say, a lot more.

When I suggest you show your child the same respect as you would an adult, I believe you should also be given the same respect back. Usually, if you show respect, you will see it reflected. However, sometimes that is not the case. It could be due to external influences or a phase the child is going through. As parents, we have to guide our children on the importance of respecting another being, whoever it may be. So, whether this means inculcating a certain amount of discipline in their routine, which they might not agree with, or expecting them to handle their tempers or discuss issues in private, as parents we should expect them to understand and explain these things to them.

As parents, we do need to set certain boundaries and explain why they should respect our advice as it comes from love. This also helps them learn self-control, which we sometimes forget will help our children be happier in the long run.

Sometimes, we as parents fall into extremes and allow just about anything. While we don't let anyone else disrespect us, we accept even the rudest behavior from our children. Maybe it is something they have picked up due to external or internal situations, however, it is our duty to ensure they are respectful of others and have a certain amount of self-control. When we discuss things with them and teach them the value of things, respect for people and our blessings, we are helping them to be happier adults. While we are not their Bosses, as parents we must inculcate values we deem important and it starts at this early age.

So, dear parents, your children might be smaller in size than you and they might ask you the same questions over and over again, but that by no means implies that they deserve to be treated with less respect. The word itself signifies the act of showing consideration and admiring or valuing someone for who he/she is. We already feel that way for our kids, so why not just let them know it? It's not that we don't respect them already; we just need to make sure we are more consistent in our reactions because in our busy lives we may tend to forget sometimes. If you want a confident and happy child who treats you with love and respect, try this way. I promise you, it works like magic!

Be Happy Tips

1. A child deserves the same, if not more, respect and consideration than you give your friends and family.
2. Inform your child of what you have planned for him/her, as you would any family member.
3. Inform your child of your plans as well.
4. Be honest with him/her.

5. Be conscious of the child's self-image in front of others.
6. Care about embarrassing him/her as much as you would yourself.
7. Expect and ensure you are respected, as also the boundaries you have set for your child.

WORRIED ABOUT ANGER MANAGEMENT?

It's a normal emotion

Anybody can become angry – that is easy, but to be angry with the right person and to the right degree and at the right time and for the right purpose, and in the right way – that is not within everybody's power and is not easy. ~ Aristotle

Anger is a normal emotion. It's us experiencing the ups and downs of being human. And anger in children is also normal. How we handle our anger, and how we work with our children to handle this emotion, is what is important. We should try to avoid anger in front of children. The degree to which they display this emotion is determined, to a large extent, by what they see their primary caregivers do. However, it is only natural for everyone to feel angry. But here are some useful ways to handle this emotion.

Between parent and child

Accept it as natural and remind yourself that either way you love each other very much, and the feeling is momentary. Hug your child, calm down and then react or get a point across. In a few minutes you will be reminded of the many joys this experience brings, and the anger will melt away. If sometimes you see children hitting, doing the same back to them does not help. You are only reinstating that hitting in anger is okay.

Instead, stop them, but tell them, "I would never hit you, and would you like it if I did?" Children are exposed to so many situations and people, they are bound to pick up habits we don't approve of, and how we handle these can help improve or worsen this habit.

Between parents and others

Try keeping this away from the child as far as possible. Give yourself time to cool off. Reacting in anger never achieves much good.

Bird language

In one of the seminars (Infant Siddha Program) I took, they suggested the technique of using bird language. So basically you discuss this concept with the child and follow it yourself as well. How it works is like this. If you are just a little angry, think you have a small bird on your head. If you are very angry, think you have a big bird on your head. So at your angriest you have an ostrich on your head. Then as time lapses and your anger subsides, image the ostrich has flown off, and now you have a flamingo, then an eagle, then maybe a pigeon, and then finally, as your anger is pretty much done and in control, you probably are left with just a little sparrow on your head, which eventually flies away and takes with it all your sadness and anger. This helps make the anger external and not a part of you. Plus, imagining it flying off helps in actually disassociating yourself from it, and bit by bit getting it off your chest. Plus, it's a lot better than breaking things or stomping off, isn't it? Now for this to work you have to keep talking to the child about this method, follow it yourself, and at times talk the process out loud so your child feels you are following it, even if you are only doing so for him or her to learn.

Meditation

This is a personal favorite. Yep, I really think this can be taught to kids from a very young age. There are hundreds of ways of meditation. Really by meditating I mean just focusing on your breath—trying to breathe calmly, taking longer deep breaths etc. It makes you focus on something calming such as your breath, gives your body more oxygen, and helps put things in perspective, and acts as a distraction. Try out different meditations that many recommend. You can learn from the many courses available, from online resources, or by working out your own breathing techniques that calm you down. Simple, deep, slow breathing works for me, and I love it.

Forgive yourself

If you do get angry, okay you're human, forgive yourself, love yourself, and realize the person feeling the worst is you! So figure out a way to make sure next time you manage to take a step back in this situation and not react in a way you will regret by using one of the above techniques.

Be Happy Tips

1. Anger is a normal emotion. How we handle it is key. Also, how we teach our children to handle it is the important part.
2. Never use physical reprimanding with your children even if they do. Just ask them if they would like it if you behaved the same.
3. Try using different techniques such as deep breathing to calm down or distract or let the angry moment pass.
4. Forgive your child and yourself, and just keep working on how to handle this emotion better for yourself.

WOW! BROCCOLI FOR DINNER!

The vegetable war—what works and why

It's bizarre that the produce manager is more important to my children's health than the pediatrician. ~ Meryl Streep

There are two common statements we've all heard as children:

- ✓ You're getting chocolates and ice cream today. Wow!
- ✓ You must eat your vegetables.

We can immediately associate these words with our childhoods. 'If you sleep on time, you'll get to eat ice cream!', is another such promise, as is, 'If you finish your assignments before 7pm, you'll get a chocolate from mommy! How cool is that?'.

There are numerous such enticements that parents employ to reward their little ones for good deeds and commendable efforts. However, have you ever wondered why children consider chocolates and ice creams as rewards? Glance at the two statements above. Do you notice that, unintentionally, ice cream has been made to sound like a treat, and vegetables a stern necessity? The perception of the prized item (whatever it may be… candy, cake etc), is created in young minds only after we, the parents, make them sound exciting. Because ice cream is presented with happiness, children start associating it with good things. They start believing that sweet things are delicious and prized.

Now recall how you have usually seen parents approach their children with green, leafy vegetables. 'You have to finish your vegetables. They are good for you and will make you stronger,' is what some say. At times, there is even a tone of fear reflecting, 'How do I convince them to eat this? I hope they like the taste'. There is no thrill or excitement attached to these items. No 'wow' or 'yummy!' follows. This is why children grow skeptical and when approached with a plate of veggies, they tend to feel hesitant. We are responsible for creating these associations.

If you reverse this trend, you will realize your vegetable war will come to a peaceful end before you know it. Try not to shower so much attention and awe on cakes, ice creams, and candy. I know children will always be surrounded by people who will probably do exactly that, but then you can balance it out by upping the level of excitement in your tone and expressions when it comes to vegetables. And don't waste any time in this matter, start right at the beginning as soon as your baby starts consuming solids. Here is how I tackled the vegetable war.

Introduction to solids

When solids are first introduced into a baby's diet, most parents tend to start with softer and sweeter flavours like apple stew. Since all moms and dads want to start the baby's solid feeding on a good note, they feel they should initiate the process with something yummy. What I suggest you do is inculcate the taste of vegetables early. Introduce a veggie that isn't necessarily sweet, in this phase, and make sure you express loads of excitement while doing so. You can start with any vegetables that are light and easy to digest. You'll notice that your smile is enough to get your baby to start lapping it all up!

Of course, you should first discuss with your pediatrician what exactly you can start your little one on. I remember my doctor giving me a crucial tip when I was about to start my son on solids: to make it as easy as possible for the baby. Instead of going gaga on sweet foods during this stage, try making a mash out of some handpicked vegetables. Secondly, don't throw everything you have lined up for the meal into a mixer to make an extra-soft mix. Instead, hand-mash the vegetables after boiling/steaming/cooking them as recommended by your pediatrician. Children should get used to chewing a little and feeling different textures in their mouths; that way the transition to other food will be easier. I have noticed that if you start feeding your child finely ground dishes, you will find it harder to get them started on normal meals.

This strategy has worked for every new mother I have spoken to. It's important to understand that at this stage in a child's life, anything new is a treat! Everything you feed the child will have a novel texture and will taste entirely different from the mommy's milk he/she has been living on for months. So make every food item sound exciting, and you'll begin to notice the change in your child's reactions to those food items. The child will love everything you serve. Seriously, it's that easy! Happy feeding!

New global food

Whenever you're about to introduce your baby to something new that his/ her taste buds might take a little time to get used to, be sure that you create a lot of hype around it. Kids like to feel they're in on something that everyone is talking about (might seem like a mature sentiment to develop, but take my word for it, they feel it). First and most importantly, make your child believe that what you're feeding him/her is something that you already are a massive fan of. Tell him/ her you love it, so your child knows that the two people he/ she trusts the most in life, are also crazy about this...Chinese, Japanese or other new cuisine or dish

Secondly, let children know that getting to eat this 'new food' is a privilege of sorts. Only very lucky, good and special people get to eat it. Then serve them a small portion so they don't feel the pressure of having to finish all the food. Since the quantity looks eatable, their curiosity will convince them to try it and see it in a good light. Also, be careful in moments when you think your child isn't watching you or listening to what you are saying. At that impressionable age, he/she will automatically imbibe what they see their most trusted family members doing. Refrain from making faces or criticizing foods unnecessarily, or you'll soon see them following suit. Probably that's why my friends think I'm bonkers sometimes. Every time my son and I order salad at dinner, we pretty much do a back flip on the arrival of our meal. Who expects that from a four-year-old? Hey, but isn't that better than trying to trick your child into eating some hidden nutrients?

Less means more

As funny as it may seem, the saying 'abstinence makes the heart grow fonder', doesn't only apply to couples in love. It works for vegetables too! Seriously. I know this technique works purely because I've seen myself craving cheesecake every time I'm on a diet. And man, does it taste like heaven when I treat myself to some at the end of a 45-day regimen. So for dinner this week, sauté some mushrooms in olive oil and let your child have a tiny, weeny bite. Then if he/she asks for more, you just might be able to give the child a bit more. If the demand comes for the third time, then congratulate yourself and then continue dishing it out. Wondering what you should congratulate yourself for? For making your child ask for more vegetables, silly!

Eating out

How often have you noticed parents ordering entirely different meals for children when they're out for dinner at a restaurant? Quite often? And if they don't, then they invite surprised looks from everyone else at the table. But we try not to do that. Unless my husband and I are ordering something extremely spicy, we always call for dishes that the entire family can gorge on. I have always maintained that our son will eat what we eat and therefore experience all varieties. So if it's vegetable pizza on the menu, that's what he will lap up. And he really does eat everything we do, making it a win-win situation for all – everyone at the table gets more variety to share, my little boy experiences different and new flavors, and his taste buds get some exercise.

Don't be afraid to experiment. Invariably, and sometimes out of habit, parents end up choosing safe/common dishes when it comes to eating out with their children. But I realized there is no point in living with the worry of what my child will think or how he will react to new foods. Did I mention he loves broccoli? Well, he does! Every time my son sits up as his bowl of vegetables, fruit, or salad arrives at the table, there is this general sense of awe from the people around him. I know how amazing that feels. To top that, he actually insists on finishing his portion too. He loves it all. And I love him for the fact.

The satisfaction that you, as a parent, receive when you watch your boy/girl gobble up the vitamin and protein-laden meal that will make him/her muscles strong, is unparalleled. The compliments, however, should never stop. I make sure every time our son finishes his greens, I remind him that his strong bones and alert mind will help him build his own toy car one day (he's currently obsessed with racing miniature four-wheelers around the house). I remind him that as he grows, the advantages of eating right will help him run faster, play better, and stay fitter!

Relate children's good eating habits to the activity you know they enjoy the most. That'll give them that extra motivation to continue chomping! From their favourite cartoon characters to the people they admire around them, associate everyone's good qualities with their well-rounded and nutritious meals. The only caveat here is if the child has any food allergies. Then, of course, their bodies will reject that food automatically, for which the signs will be apparent.

Eating at home

How often have you seen parents cooking multiple meals for lunch? I know many who do. The belief is that children can be picky. As a result, sometimes you can get bogged down with the task of making them special meals, and then cooking something completely different for your husband/wife. Pets and their food is another things to take care of. At the end of the day, it all comes down to you slogging at the stove. I truly admire those parents who do find the time in their hectic lives to cater to so many demands. My husband did it too. More than just making my son happy, he would find the process of spending a few hours in the kitchen away from his workplace a de-stressor. That was great and absolutely fine. But when more often than not, our son started expecting him to cook for him something different from what we were having, I figured there might be a problem. I realized that we were ourselves setting a pattern of different foods for everyone and making it more difficult for ourselves. So we decided to get back to our much simpler and fairer practice of everyone having the same meal. We insisted our son eat what we ate, and why shouldn't he? When we attempted cooking something hot and spicy (which actually has no health benefit), we would keep a non-spicy portion for him aside. He got used to this system in no time. More importantly, the child will feel good that he/she is part of a meal the entire family shares together. The only way we were able to achieve this was by setting a precedent at an early age. As for my husband and I, we discovered that we were able to spend more hours together as a unit when we weren't toiling in the kitchen. Ending the day without some heavy-duty 'us' time is never a good idea; hugs are medicinal and magical, trust me!

So next time you step out for dinner, order for your child what you are having. If you start maintaining this simple rule at home as well, children too, will get used to the idea. Of course, every now and then, we all love pampering our children with their favorite dishes. Children deserve to devour their special treats once in a while. But make that a disciplined system. Tell your little one that every Saturday, he/she can request a dish they want.

Children are not born picky. They become picky after they notice us, their parents, reacting positively or negatively to certain foods. If your children have heard you say, "Don't give them vegetable pizza, they may not like it", you'll notice that they will start avoiding it. If you hadn't planted the thought in their brains, they may have actually liked it. Remember, every minute you spend with your children is important and will shape the way they think. Children are always watching and looking up to their parents, so they imbibe their qualities too. That's another reason why you should refrain from making any strong and negative comments about any food. If children hear you say, "Yuck! That tastes horrible," then they'll react to a taste they don't prefer in the same overtly negative manner. And that's the last thing you want. If something tastes odd or bad, simply say, "I think this has gone bad". Avoid using negative words like 'yuck' or 'horrible'. In fact, try not to use such negative words for anything. This habit can play an instrumental part in forming children's eating habits. Even if one parent, or someone else, does not eat certain foods, we should try not to point it out. Even in passing, children hear, 'Oh, dad has never liked vegetables'. They will take that as normal and may emulate that parent by not eating vegetables as well. So any negative connotations and conversations should be avoided. We have to consciously protect our children from our own limitations.

These techniques can also be used with fruits, not just with vegetables. In fact, adapting them to make sure your child eats bananas and berries, is much easier. Because so many of them taste sweet, children associate fruits with fun food. I have implemented all the above-mentioned techniques as a mother. As a result, my boy eats his nutrient-packed meals every day and my husband and I have more free. You will also know that when your child needs to travel the world, he/ she will never have an issue finding food.

A friend of mine recently called me from Malaysia and spent 15 minutes telling me how there wasn't any vegetarian food there. I've been to Malaysia and found great food, as I told him. The truth was that he didn't like what he ate there because he had never developed a taste for world cuisine and new foods when he was young. My son has been travelling the world with us ever since he was two months old. In India he eats lentils, rice, and vegetables. He also loves fondu and fish and chips. Salads and soups bring a big smile to his face, as do hotdogs and burgers, and dishes with cherry tomatoes are his all-time favourites. In other parts of Asia, he'll merrily slurp into his bowl of noodles. Travelling with my little jet-setter is never stressful. I hope you use the techniques enumerated in this chapter to help you make the most of your next family vacation. Enjoy the feeling of knowing your child is getting to experience the delightful joys of good food.

Be Happy Tips

1. Show as much or more excitement for savoury and healthy foods such as fruits and vegetables as you show for ice cream and chocolates.
2. While introducing solids, first introduce savoury tastes.
3. Make vegetables a treat from the beginning, and you will see children eating them happily.
4. Maintain the same meals for children and adults.
5. Don't restrict your children's food by always ordering the same dish for them. Always order the same foods for everyone when you go out or travel.
6. Let children experiment and experience new foods from an early age, to help them develop a taste for different foods.
7. Never use words like 'yuck' or 'ugh' or impose your own limitations and likes/dislikes about food, on your children. Avoid mentioning your limitations.

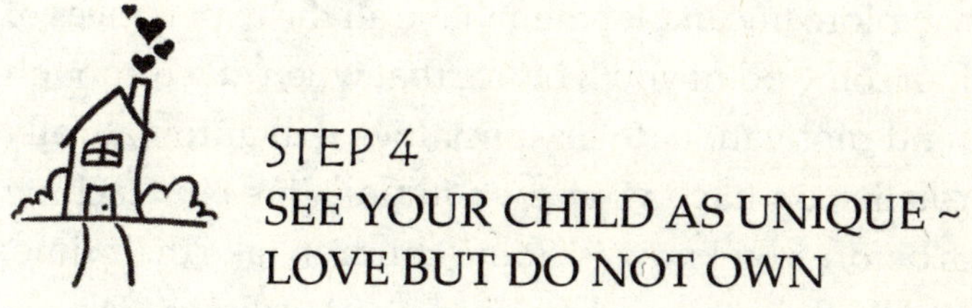

STEP 4

SEE YOUR CHILD AS UNIQUE ~ LOVE BUT DO NOT OWN

DON'T FORCE THE TIGER TO FLY!

Every child is a genius

Everybody is a genius. But if you judge a fish by its ability to climb a tree, it will spend its whole life thinking it's stupid.

~ Albert Einstein

It was Albert Einstein who made this statement many years ago. And it is true. Every child is indeed a genius! Even the ones who don't listen to Beethoven's compositions are prodigies in their own right. All children are special in their own unique ways. You will see glimpses of this fact in their innocent but ingenious questions or in their simple techniques of dealing with life. We've all witnessed their spark. Some parents feel the ability to learn alphabets and numbers faster than usual makes their children special. Others consider being able to read at the age of two, commendable. These achievements are worth being proud of but being special is not limited to a select few, because every child is a genius. Your child is special.

Children will eventually figure out what they are meant to do, what they will be and what they have the best skill set for. We just need to provide them with the environment to get in touch with their inner masterminds. Give children loads of love and be there for them when they need you. We need to help them explore life and let them have all the experiences of the world. At some point you'll notice that when given enough exposure and motivation, their specialties will automatically surface. You'll soon have your own junior Einstein teaching you things before you know it! Some children take their time, but eventually they themselves find their callings. We, as their strongest support system, can help them discover their goals and further their processes by standing by them. All we can give them in these growing years is lots of love, positive reinforcement, and motivation.

I have constantly stressed the need to avoid negativity, in many of the preceding sections. If you continue to shun negative thoughts and actions, you will ensure your child's creative streaks are not dampened. It is essential that we not force our beliefs on children. If they are allowed to spread their wings and discover their own meanings to life, they will be able to spot their specialties with a lot more ease. Children who are encouraged to be open-minded and given a lot of confidence in their formative years, grow up to be more secure, happier, and charismatic. They take initiatives without worrying all the time and are in general more comfortable with their own identities.

Of course, there will be moments when you will feel you have spotted the ultimate skill set in your child. At such times, you should encourage the child to continue pursuing it. But don't tag him/her just yet. The specific ability that you may have noticed, may be a fraction of what is to follow. For instance, if you see your child humming a certain tune, don't jump to the conclusion, 'Oh, my son/daughter should become a singer!'. Instead, let that talent develop further. For all you know, the child might actually be interested in playing an instrument and might be even better at that!

Getting into another aspect of this, renowned Indian author Gurcharan Das's book, *The Difficulty of Being Good*, in some parts explains this predicament well. He delves into the two sides of every coin, in an attempt to explain dilemmas. For some reason, the world over, children tend to get easily tagged as being 'too naughty', 'too talkative', or 'lazy'. Sometimes, even educated teachers in school, which is where the most enlightened methods of teaching are implemented, tend to fall into this trap. It's very easy for children to get branded in these years. I too, got tagged as 'too talkative', and others as 'very stubborn'. But have you ever realized that all these connotations probably have positive aspects? Only fast thinkers with active minds can manage to talk a lot, and those who are persistent and driven in life can sometimes be misinterpreted as being stubborn. Sometimes you think, 'My child just doesn't listen to me'. But have you ever asked yourself whether you are being crystal clear in what you are expecting of him/her? Maybe the child is just trying to figure out the logic behind what you are saying. And you'll notice that the moment the child understands, he/she will immediately act upon it.

When you label children, you make them believe that they are being reprimanded for their behavior in some way. And that can really harm the development of their personalities. Let them be free. Don't contain them within these tags (unless positive), and you will notice that their unique qualities will inevitably show themselves. They have a right to our respect. Take your time to understand your child's temperament and what works for him/her. You know the child the best. Remember, there are always two sides to a coin. All you have to do is flip it over to discover the magic. And the advantages, let me assure you, are endless. Your children will always try to reflect or prove your positive interpretation of their behaviour right. Your constructive outlook will help them develop their self-image. When children are not cornered in any way, the chances of them discovering their unique talents are very high. This discovery or realization will only help them grow into more confident human beings. They will lead more fulfilling lives after discovering their actual calling. And any career that is born out of intrinsic talent and true passion, is far more satisfying!

There will also be moments when you will try to figure out what your children are good at simply by observing their behaviour and interests. Let me warn you, this can be a tricky task. For instance, if your child is attempting to put together a jigsaw puzzle, but isn't succeeding, don't think, 'I don't think my son/daughter will be interested in brainteasers'. Instead, notice that the child's repeated efforts actually highlight different qualities altogether –patience and perseverance – which, if you ask me, are great tools to achieve success in life!

Be Happy Tips

1. Don't label your child. Calling him/her naughty, talkative, inattentive, disobedient, or bratty, will only curb the development of the child's personality. See the positive aspects of these traits and celebrate them.
2. Your child is a genius! Don't ever let anyone or any other kid's behaviour convince you otherwise.
3. Be happy for your children. Give them time to find their calling, and you will see that their magical qualities will naturally stand out and shine bright, and this will let them lead truly fulfilling lives.

LOVE YOUR CHILD FROM HEAD TO TOE!

Building self-confidence

Work hard to create in your child a good self-image. It's the most important thing you can do to insure their success. ~ Life's Little Instruction Book

Loving your child is very important. I know this is the last thing any parent needs to be told, but the point I want to stress in this section is about telling this to children verbally and unconditionally. We all love our children and dedicate our entire lives to them. But informing them of this time unconditionally and again, is important. I've reinforced this fact throughout the book because I realize how much this means to little kids. They need to know that they are being adored every minute of their lives. You have to tell them that you love them when they are happy, when they are sad, unusually quiet, usually noisy, heartily laughing, sobbing and crying, cheery and joyful, and even when they are stubborn and grumpy. Don't forget to say those three magic words, *I love you*, even when they're angry! That's when they need to hear it a lot, actually. We can help them handle anger better and not base our love on it. In fact, pause in the middle of doing something, stop and look them in the eye and tell them you LOVE them.

One is loved because one is loved. No reason is needed for loving. ~ Paul Coelho

It is very natural for children to exhibit all kinds of emotions and they need to know we are there for them irrespective of what mood they are in or what mistakes they have made. Everything in the world comes with terms and conditions, but our love for our children goes beyond all restrictions. They should know that.

Sometimes, telling them that you love every part of them also helps give them confidence. Many times, I hear parents say things like, 'Oh, my son is too short', or 'My daughter's hair isn't that great'. Statements like these can cause irrevocable damage. Tell your children that you love their hands, fingers, toes, nose, eyes, hair, and feet… Let no part of them be left out! I also plant a soft kiss as I say this. You will enjoy seeing your child's reaction and will love telling my son how special and gorgeous he is, and how perfect he is. While telling him this, I make sure I also put in lots of positive affirmations such as, 'I love the beautiful heart you have' to 'I love the adorable nose you have'. I also tell him how he's perfect and the best gift the world could have given me and that I love him unconditionally.

Knowing that they always have us to fall back upon will give them the strength and security to pursue the challenges of life more easily. They will feel complete and happy, which is exactly what we want them to be. When your child looks to you for comfort in a crowded room, be ready with a smile on your face. When he/she comes to you after hours of playing in the field, keep your arms open and hugs prepared. After all, isn't that what families are there for? When you need a hug, that's where you should be able to go.

It is our responsibility, as the older and wiser ones, to ensure the young ones are secure and have self-confidence. Along with showering them with love, also remember to share laughs with your children as many times as you can and more! They need to know that you are always there to make things better. Reinforce the fact that you will try your best to ensure that there is nothing in life that can bring a frown to their faces as long as you are around. If you make a mistake, laugh loudly at yourself. If they go wrong, be compassionate about it, and if they are comfortable, laugh it out *with* them, not *at* them. They should know that you are on their team and that human beings do make mistakes sometimes. Nothing is the end of the world. Life is full of opportunities for them to learn and improve.

The great thing about laughing for no apparent reason is that it takes away the stress from situations. After which, dealing with the situation becomes simpler. If it is a goof-up, then the seriousness melts away with the giggles, after which communication is a lot easier. The matter can then be discussed with love and not sadness, regret, or fear. The more you laugh, the deeper grows your connection. You know what they say, laughter is indeed the best medicine.

I know that some of you must be wondering, will all this doting not result in spoilt children? Will it not hinder inculcating good habits? Will it demotivate them from growing into better human beings? Will it not make them take certain people for granted? Well, the answer is *no*. Look at the bigger picture. For instance, instead of only saying, 'I love you for getting such good grades', we should say, 'I love you for trying your best' or 'I love you because you tried so well and so hard to learn new things' or 'I love you, always'. If you follow all the tips mentioned in this book, you will see that by setting an example, your children will reflect the best of what they have learnt from you. They will grow up to be sensitive, loving, caring and conscientious. And the bonus is that by reaffirming we love everything about our children, they will develop more confidence and a good self-image. Aren't those some of the most essential characteristics to have in life?

Be Happy Tips

1. Love and see the beauty of *every* physical aspect of your child and make sure you tell him/her that regularly.
2. The love you feel for your children is unconditional. Let them know you are there for them no matter what mood they are in.
3. Laugh with your kid whenever you can. You will see that just ejecting the seriousness from a situation always makes it easier for children to understand and communicate.

PROMOTE NATURAL CURIOSITY WITHIN SAFE BOUNDARIES !

Experience-based learning

A major part of parenting involves looking out for your child's safety. The moment children leave your sight, there is constant worry. Even when they are around us, we're on high alert and persistently hoping they don't hurt themselves, whether sipping hot soup or running down a stairwell too fast. It's only natural to be tense. We never want our children to feel an ounce of discomfort and we are ready to go to bizarre lengths to protect them. Sometimes, when I look around even at my own house, I notice so many dangers lurking that a child can fall prey to. But then I make a conscious point to remind myself that my son will eventually have to walk out into the world and deal with all these situations himself. What's the point of always being harrowed? We might be able to save our children from tripping over an uneven tile or an untied shoelace, but will we always be around to combat the stresses they face later in life? As much as I would love to, I don't think so. Our children will eventually move out of the nest and will have to deal with their troubles themselves. What we can do is help them develop an understanding of how to manage those situations.

I am going to share with you a few tips that will ease this process for you. At the same time, that does not mean we stop taking precautions and become careless. Always make all your final judgments and decisions based on what your doctors and counsellors say. Their recommendations and our understanding are equally essential. But the techniques outlined here have worked. I have seen their effects first-hand.

If your toddler asks for your permission to attempt something that is potentially dangerous, your intrinsic reaction is to say no! And that is understandable. But what I said previously about not saying no, still stands. The moment you prohibit your child from doing something, he/she will want to do exactly that, more than ever. That's why children sometimes need to experience things to understand the significance of our fears and skepticism. Of course, this does not mean that we should falter in taking necessary precautionary measures.

For instance, when you place a hot dish on the dinner table, your first reaction is to ask your child to be careful and refrain from touching it. However, your kid will continue to feel curious. I know this may sound tough, but I suggest you allow him/her to give it a fleeting touch in a controlled environment, just so they can understand the gravity of your statement. Children will then reach the conclusion that a just-cooked dish can be hot and harmful if touched. Let the child feel a sharp corner gently to understand that if they run towards it too fast, they face the chance of being harmed. They will realize that these feelings aren't comforting and pleasant, and therefore, in future they will be careful about such situations even when you are not with them. They will logically be able to gauge a hazard. Explain that in your absence they have to keep these senses on high alert. And you will see your children automatically become careful. No one likes getting hurt.

Of course, this strategy can't work for everything or for children of all ages. When you ask your infant not to touch a lit lamp or stick a finger into an electric plug point, even though the child may want to do so, you obviously cannot permit it. There is an appropriate amount of experience-based teaching that you can provide to your children at different ages. But once you feel your children are old enough to understand what you mean to achieve by letting them experience situations, don't stop them from doing certain things without giving them a logical justification or reason for your disapproval. The more you control what your children want to do, the more they will want to do it. It's a proven theory; you know it. When we're told not to eat pizza, what is the one thing we crave the most? Pizza! Even though we feel children need to be warned and taken care of, they also need to have first-hand experiences with life. Not only does it help them develop free and independent thought, but also makes them responsible.

Allow children to reach their own conclusions. Facilitate an environment wherein they can understand why certain activities can prove harmful, using experience-based teaching. In situations where actual experiences can prove harmful, talk to your children. Question them on how they would feel if they touched the burning flame of a candle. Give them reference points so they can compare situations. Then wait for them to answer, and you will see that they will automatically understand. Children are very bright.

This same methodology can be utilized when it comes to discovering your children's inner talent too. In order to make the right decision, it is important to understand all the options available. Only then can we make an informed decision, which is why you shouldn't force your children into taking up careers or interests that you, personally, like. Let them participate in different sports, play various instruments, and study a variety of subjects. Then let them decide what makes them happy. After all, no matter what happens, it is their happiness that is of paramount significance.

Your role in this process is that of a facilitator and motivator. At every step, you have to stand by their experiments, provide them with all that they need to carry out those trials, and then appreciate them for their smallest and greatest achievements. They will look to you for approval and will always try to impress you, so make sure you don't set unrealistic goals or expectations. I have explained previously how you can make your children love vegetables. All you have to do is be excited about a plate of greens. If you walk up to them with some nutritious veggies and make the meal sound like it is as exciting as a tub of ice cream, they will naturally love to indulge. You have to play a similar part while helping your children gather experiences and knowledge of the world. Your words mean everything to them, so remember to use them wisely.

When I was young, I remember my parents speaking highly about the son of a family friend, who had gone abroad to study. I would hear them talk about him often. As a result, I began to believe that leaving the country for further studies was something my mother and father truly valued. I was convinced that if I did the same thing, they would be equally proud of me. So, a few years later, I brought up the subject and discussed the idea of going overseas. In fact, my parents didn't feel it was the best idea for me to leave India at that age. They did not realize that it was they who had planted in me the desire to excel in a school abroad. With parenting comes the great power to be able to guide a living being's life in the right direction.

So if you feel your son/daughter will really enjoy learning how to play the piano, then expose him/her to the beauty of the instrument. Take your child to concerts, try learning the instrument yourself, and practice it with the child when the opportunity presents itself. If you try to force children into learning to play the piano, the lessons will become a task for them and will no longer be fun. The learning will get hindered, and the process will become purely about following orders from parents who they respect and would not like to disappoint. They will not value the art, nor will they feel motivated to excel at it. If you develop an interest in it yourself and make your excitement evident, then they too, will start taking what you have to say seriously. And you will see that if your kid is truly interested, he/she will definitely reciprocate the thrill of your recommendation. If children continue to exhibit disinterest towards that particular activity, understand this, they are still waiting to find their actual calling. And it's only a matter of time and exposure till your child, and you, figure out what it is.

It is in the early years that children also learn about the five senses. It is important they develop a keen understanding of smell, touch, sight, taste, and sound. Take them for a walk in the park and let them smell the flowers. Try to teach them about nature through these trips. They can be exposed to something that smells minty, fruity or even burnt. Once in a while, make sure they accompany you to buy groceries so they can touch and feel various textures of fruits and vegetables. The more the variety, the stronger their body of experiences will be.

Though their eyes are constantly at work, being exposed to the world and its sights, also take them to art exhibitions every now and then. Appreciating a painting is a very different kind of learning. As for tastes, allow them to eat dishes that are salty, sweet, sour, and even a little spicy, though you might want to keep a glass of water handy for the last one. Encourage them to tap different surfaces to create various noises. Play soothing music that, you feel, will help them inculcate a taste for quality sound. Effectively using all their senses will help them throughout their lives. And there is something in it for you too. When you walk into a restaurant and watch your child proclaim enthusiastically, "I smell cheese!", you will smile, unable to describe that magical feeling!

Be Happy Tips

1. Stressing and worrying all the time about dangers lurking around your kids is not going to help. Instead, when you're in a controlled environment, help them understand and gently experience the threat those dangers pose, by letting them feel the sharp corner of a shelf etc. They will identify with your fears logically and be twice as cautious in your absence. This will be more effective and save you a lot of stress.
2. If you are convinced that your children could be great at certain things, expose them to the options wholeheartedly. But don't push them into things. Let them discover everything with the help of first-hand fun experiences. Let them make informed decisions.
3. Make an effort to help your children experience the five senses in different ways. It really helps.

BOO-BOOS ARE GOOD!

Physical development

It is paradoxical that many educators and parents still differentiate between a time for learning and a time for play without seeing the vital connection between them.

~ Leo F. Buscaglia

Children love playing. Running around and swinging from branches is what they do when they are young. I'm sure you did too. And where there is activity involved, there is always the chance of a slip or a trip. But that's all part of growing up. Let your kids go crazy! Racing, jumping, and even falling, contributes to the child's physical development. All this not only gives children a chance to release their pent-up energy, but also helps strengthen their muscles and develop balance.

Yes, it is our responsibility as parents to protect them, but don't do so by prohibiting them in any way. We all have our fears but that does not mean our children should feel afraid of the same things. I am usually brave and open-minded when it comes to our son's playtime. I never hold him back when he's out on the field. But a few years ago, I had one fear – horses. Like every parent, I wanted my son to learn to ride and have his share of fun. But I would feel scared when he was around them because I had faced a frightening experience. Since then, I had not got over my panic around horses. Many years ago, while on vacation with my family, I was seated on a horse. We were riding up a hill when the horse lost its balance. I was thrown off. I managed to escape being trampled by inches. It was a terrifying experience. Even though I made it a point to accompany my son to the stable, and I also encouraged him to learn to ride, deep down inside I would be dealing with a million knots in my stomach. As much as I tried to fight the thoughts with a smile on my face, I kept imagining my son's safety being compromised. As a result, he started noticing the apprehension in my tone, and then my fear got transferred onto him. He too, began feeling scared and refused to go back to the stable.

Then my mother noticed the situation and spoke to me. She explained that accidents are rare and what happened with me was a freak case. I began to understand that my fear was holding my son back from experiencing something new. So I corrected myself. I began making a conscious effort to shove the scary thoughts out of my mind. I reminded myself of how much fun riding a horse used to be before that dread incident took place. And soon enough, my positivity changed my son's mind too. On his own he asked if we could go to the racecourse again. The technique of associating joy with situations you want your children to think are fun, works like magic. If your children see you happily playing in the rain or swimming in the sea, they too, will consider those activities enjoyable.

A dear friend of mine, who is the mother of a baby girl, was petrified when someone told her a story about a toddler drowning in a pool. Naturally, after hearing horror tales when things went drastically wrong, any parent would be worried about letting his/her child go near a swimming pool. I explained to her that if she was always with her daughter when she was learning how to swim in the kiddy pool, there would be no scope for a mishap. It would be completely safe. She too, after a lot of counseling, was able to get over her fears. Now she loves sitting by the pool watching her daughter splash around in glee. A keen involvement in physical activities such as sports, also helps children learn to strategize, work within a team, and play fairly. All these qualities add to the development of a child's personality.

Make it a point to travel with your children. Many parents feel that taking children to new countries may compromise their immune systems and increase the chances of infections, or just mess up their routines. But none of that is true. My son has been travelling with us since he was 20 days old. When he was three, we took him to Singapore. He missed a few days of kindergarten and many people called us 'weird' and 'irresponsible'. They even asked us, "Where do you think he would learn more—three days in school or in Singapore?" You can only imagine what my response to that question was. We didn't care about those comments and my son came back hopping and skipping with glee. In those few days he had seen an entire country, met new people, tried out different foods (and loved almost all of what he ate), and had experiences that taught him a lot. He was happy. I was glad.

As for a child's immune system (something many parents worry about), well, apparently when children are exposed to germs, their bodies only get stronger as they learn how to fight the infections. Slowly and steadily, the body develops stronger immunity and is able to ward off germs much more efficiently.

Make the most of these first few years of your child's life. There are no examinations in school that you or your child need to worry about, nor are there any difficult books that you have to help them read. Take the children out with you wherever you go, so that they can learn from all that is around them. Break the monotony and you will see that they will grow up to be more adjusting human beings. Interestingly, stepping out can also help your children excel in school. Rather than showing them pictorial books about birds and animals, take them to the zoo and point out the real creatures. Let them observe the animals and learn everything there is to know about their lives. Doesn't that sound so much better than staring at photographs in a book? You can follow the same technique when they're learning about nature. Take your children on garden walks. Allow them to run around the park, smell the flowers, touch and climb the trees, and run after tiny insects. There is an awful lot to be learnt from the wonderful world around us.

Be Happy Tips

1. Let your child run, jog, walk, and fall. Physical activity is very important. It makes children stronger, more flexible, and improves balance.
2. Don't force your fears onto your children. They should not have to think twice about something they want to do, just because you had a negative experience.
3. Children learn a lot through play; in fact, if you want to make learning fun, make it experience-based or a game.
4. Your children always look up to you. If you show them how much you enjoy the wide world, they will develop an interest in the outdoors as well. Doing so helps your children remain healthy and fit. It also combats the craze for the Internet and the tube.

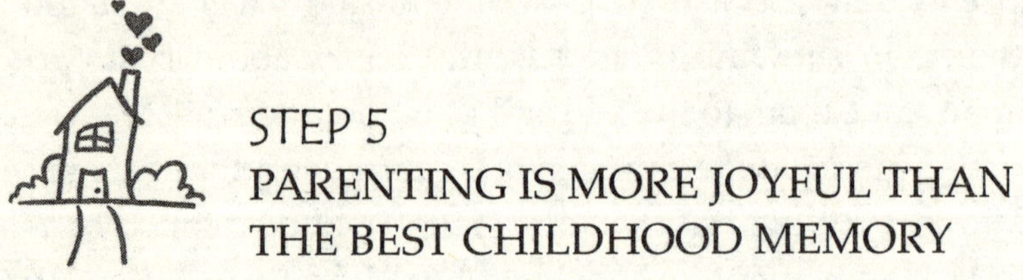

STEP 5
PARENTING IS MORE JOYFUL THAN THE BEST CHILDHOOD MEMORY

YOUR OWN PIECE OF HEAVEN

Children are gifts; learn from them

No one has yet fully realized the wealth of sympathy, kindness and generosity hidden in the soul of a child. The effort of every true education should be to unlock that treasure.

~ Emma Goldman

A child is the greatest blessing nature can gift you. To even attempt to describe the joy that parents experience in their lifetime as they watch their little ones grow, would be impossible. It is truly indescribable. Sometimes, in our daily rush, we forget to appreciate the small pleasures that life grants us. But I urge you to make the most of all those moments. Follow this checklist to let every inch of your being enjoy parenthood.

1. Cherish your child. Becoming a mother or father is the best thing that can happen to you.
2. Hug your children as much and as many times as you can. There is no such thing as too much love.
3. Learn from your children. Remember, they look at life in a manner that will forever be new for us.
4. Enjoy every moment. Relish their little jokes and misadventures. Laugh with them.
5. Your child is a present. Thank him/her for being such a beautiful being.

I have elaborated upon each of the above mentioned *mantras* in the next few pages and have followed these guidelines myself. I started seeing my world from a miraculous point of view and I know you will too.

Cherish your child

Over the ages, tomes have been written to describe the thrill of bringing up a child. But to really experience that sentiment, you have to become a parent. Nothing can explain that feeling of wanting to dedicate your entire life to one priceless soul and the complete adoration that you so naturally feel for your baby. No oil paints can create a picture that is as adorable as the sight of your child resting peacefully in your arms. The love is unimaginable. Children really are gifts. We are not the ones who choose when we should become parents. Haven't you heard of people trying to conceive and finding it hard to do so? Well, that is because it is the children who decide when and how they want to enter this world and brighten it. Human beings aren't perfect, and somehow I believe that children choose their carriers based on those very flaws. So don't berate yourself or compare your child to others. Comparisons are neither complete nor justified because you never truly know what the other picture is all about.

Your baby is perfect and unique as he/she is. As a mother or father, you will experience bliss that is unimaginable, love that is unexplainable, and hugs that are irreplaceable. The affection that your child will envelope you in will suddenly give your life a purpose you didn't know existed. When I first met my husband, I was truly, madly, and deeply in love with him. I never thought that feeling could ever be replicated or bettered. But, boy was I in for a surprise! The day I held my son in my arms, all that I had believed for 25 years suddenly changed. Not that I love my husband any differently; I adore him, but trust me, this is a unique feeling. Your child will fill you up with so much love that you will be left wondering whether any other feeling can ever match it.

The bond between a parent and child is the stuff of magic. Your baby is the most loyal, loving, amazingly intelligent, creative, and hilariously funny gift nature can ever give you. Here is an example of the kind of love a child offers you. A friend was recently sitting on her balcony looking at the stars with her six-year-old son. He looked into her eyes and said, "Mom, I hope you live for 100 years and never, ever die."

I once told my son in passing, "You're so cute and make me so happy, I really don't want to you grow up"(I didn't really mean it; I love every minute of every age and phase). But he turned right back to me and said, "Mom, I will pray to God not to make me grow up fast, because I love you and want you to be happy". Is that not a moment worth remembering always and a story worth telling your grandchildren? Every parent has tons of these they can talk about and should focus on. Yes, children are a lot of work and we have to multitask a great deal between work, home, children, and a social life, but they can give you such moments of wonder and unconditional love that it makes it all worthwhile. It's up to us to focus on the love and special moments or to focus on the work involved. Eventually this choice will determine what our experience of parenting will be.

Kids are a constant source of amusement and wonder. It's up to us to cherish the time we spend with them and enjoy the minute details and their smallest achievements. Go out of your way to spend those few quality hours with them even if you are busy. You'll understand the importance of what you did when you look back many years later.

Hug them as often and as many times as you can

There's no such thing as 'too much loving'. Even though that phrase sounds more like a Beatles song, it's true. Well, so are a lot of other things they sang about; I know I love my son, *Eight Days a Week*. But I'm digressing. How often have we heard the saying, 'Don't spoil your child', or 'Don't pamper them too much'? I refuse to believe in either. Who made these guidelines, and on the basis of what? Why should we trust them?

Does giving your children a hundred hugs a day amount to spoiling them? I don't think so. Would someone call it a mistake? A big *no*! Reminding your children every day that you love them inside out only helps them feel more secure in life. They are happier because they know someone is there for them through thick and thin. And that security helps makes them conscientious. You can never spoil your child with too much love. All you can do is help children grow into stronger individuals. In the end, they will gain the confidence to walk out into the world with a lot more vigour.

Some time ago, my son confessed to me that he argued with his nanny and even said something very rude. Had I lost my temper and punished him, I could not have expected him to come up to me with such brutal honesty. He would have been scared to do so. But without anyone having told him that he had misbehaved, he poured his heart out to me. So I did what works best. I sat him down, gave him a big hug, and allowed him to narrate the entire escapade to me. He said, "Mom, I made a mistake. I was a little naughty today, but only because no one was listening to what I had to say. I was feeling really sick." I felt so sad that he had to resort to anger to be heard. He had a reason and a very valid one. I knew I had not spoilt this child. Anger is a common emotion. Remember the saying, 'To err is human'? Well it is. As long as we can admit where we went wrong and correct ourselves, it's all good.

As a matter of fact, I shared some of the most wonderful moments with my son while I was writing this book. I had dozed off near my laptop one evening. At two o'clock that night, I felt my son's presence. He was kneeling by my side. I had felt the touch of his hand, and in an instant I was wide-awake. He was gently holding my fingers. Then he began rubbing both his hands together to generate some heat and placed them on my eyes to relax me. I couldn't help myself, tears flooded my eyes. He said to me, "Mom, you've been working on the laptop for so long, your eyes must be hurting. This will help you feel better." This, my dear friends, is just a fraction of the amount of engulfing happiness a child can fill you up with.

On Sundays, when my husband and I usually have a chance to sleep in late, our son's caring attitude still surprises us. If he wakes up early, instead of disturbing us, he peeps in to see how fast asleep we are and then goes off to play for a bit on his own. Then, after some time, he comes, kisses us on our cheeks, and whispering, asks us whether we want to wake up. If we mumble (which at times we do), he tucks us right back in and goes off to give his toys company.

My husband and I sometimes give each other foot massages at the end of tough days. My son, being the curiously attentive child that he is, must have watched us do so. My husband walked in post-work recently and collapsed on the sofa, only to be recharged by my son's tiny hands busy trying to massage his feet. My husband obviously jumped out of his seat and gave my son a big hug before swirling him around in glee. We were so touched, because never have we ever asked him to do any such thing. This was all his initiative. Can you believe that, and does it sound like we had spoilt him?

I have a thousand memories of magical moments like this, and I am sure you do too. If you focus on the loving aspects of parenting and continue standing by the theories I have shared in this book, your record book of magical stories will continue overflowing with such tales.

Learn from your child's innocence

The innocence of children is amazing and infectious. Their belief that anything is possible, their multitude of questions, and their ability to see things in a different light, is something we can truly apply to our own lives in order to revive the magic of our childhoods.

I had a bad day at work and came home feeling visibly annoyed. I was exhausted and just wanted to be left alone. When my son noticed that I didn't walk in looking as excited as I usually do, he didn't throw a tantrum. Instead, he walked up to me and hugged me quietly. He did not say anything, nor was I expected to reciprocate. Thinking of that moment gets me teary eyed. Now this is a quality that we must learn from our children. So effortlessly, my son charmed my mood with his innocence. There were no preconceived notions, just love.

On another occasion, the three of us were out at a restaurant for dinner. My son was battling a bit of a cold. When we ordered soda for ourselves, we called for a glass of water for him. He asked us why he didn't get a soda as well, and we explained why. He understood but felt bad. Being the innocent soul that he was, he had a tear in his eye but quietly hid it. Aren't children just angels?

Pure love

Even though they probably only reach your knee, children are always looking out for their parents. You all know what I'm talking about here. Even if someone jokingly nudges or pokes us, they get protective. There is no judgment, just love.

Many well-meaning friends and family members sometimes jokingly ask our children this common question: 'Who do you love more – mom or dad?'. My son always responds to that query with a 'why-would-you- ask-me-such-a-peculiar-question' look on his face and says, "I love both my mom and my dad". This just proves that children feel protective of their parents even at such a young and vulnerable age. You will see very young children get upset when someone humorously slaps their parent on the back. If that isn't pure love, then what is?

Small wonders

In the constant rush to make the most of 24 hours, missing the small joys of life is easy. But children remain amazed and curious even about the simplest things. They breathe in the fragrance of every flower, watch a snail as it crawls across a tile, spot the beauty in shells on the beach, enjoy the taste of each crystal of sugar, the smell of cake, the first rains, and so on. You know the phrase 'stop and smell the roses'? Well, that's exactly what we should learn from our children. It's amazing, uplifting, and enlightening. It's a lot more fun to talk about blooming flowers or how high a frog can jump, than to rant and crib about the state of governance and politics. For a change, follow your kid's footsteps, and let him/her teach you that there is a lot more to life than meets the eye.

Whenever reminiscing, most adults recall their childhoods as the best times of their lives. Yes, those were the wonder years. But I think the ones that follow are, or can be, equally good. All we have to do is consistently live life with the same amount of curiosity that enveloped our thoughts when we were toddlers. Get in touch with your inner child. And I know that can be tough. As adults we have many more issues to take care of, so it's not always easy to switch off. I know because I've had my share of experiences too. All I think is that if we try to focus a little more on the beauty of life, dealing with those experiences will become a lot easier.

Revive the beauty of your childhood by learning from your little ones. Don't let your stresses affect your kid's view of the world. Remain open to this new way of life. And you will not be alone following this ideology. The day you start sharing your toddler's innocence and happiness, and his/her ability to feel joy at the smallest instance, you will find their little fingers holding yours and guiding you into a world of wonderment.

Enjoy every minute

Motherhood makes you smile so much. You might tire of other pursuits but never will you feel weary of the satisfaction you feel when you see your child finish a healthy meal, run fast, grow well, enjoy a book or laugh with exultation. You will also never have enough of the immense love that your child gives you. The fact that we all remember most of the special moments we have shared with our children proves that this journey never stops being exciting. Whether it is when they first attempted chewing solid foods, gave us their first kiss, the first finger clench, to expressions they wear when they're feeling mischievous and get caught, the sentiments are innumerable and indescribable. All of us have cried when our children have overwhelmed us with surprise hugs and gentle tugs. This never changes. When your children are ready to become parents themselves, you'll still feel like protecting them and holding their hands through it all.

For you, your child will always remain that cuddly bundle of joy that changed your life. It's nature at work. You will find it physically, mentally, and emotionally impossible not to love your child more with every passing day. There can be no greater learning than to love someone unconditionally. Parenting teaches us that. If you allow every moment with your child to settle in your conscience permanently, you will notice that you are a happier person.

Follow these simple *mantras*: thank them, hug them, tell them you love them very much – and you will truly enjoy the joys of parenting. You will feel like the most cherished caretaker in the world. I know because I follow these techniques. I often wonder whoever coined that silly phrase, 'being a homemaker is a thankless job'. it is the most satisfying, magical, and well-paying job I know.

Be Happy Tips

1. Cherish the great gift your child is. He/she will love you like no one can. Enjoy the beautiful moments that each day brings.
2. Hugging is therapeutic; enjoy the child's adorable hugs while he/she is at the age to love them too, and help your child be comfortable showing affection.
3. Learn from children – their innocence, wonder, positivity, and ability to laugh with happiness about the smallest things.
4. Enjoy the best gift the world can give you. There are magical joys in parenting, and remind yourself how lucky you really are for the many special moments you experience.

THANK YOUR CHILD

Demonstrate appreciation

Don't forget a person's biggest emotional need is to feel appreciated.
~ Life's Little Instruction Book

Your children give you unconditional love and re-teach you the joys of life, and help you in every way they can. They are also the reason you experience the bliss of being a parent. Children are the best gifts the universe can give you. Thank the world, and thank your children for all this. These are some of the simple courtesies we are taught when we are young – to say please, thank you, and sorry.

These same rules apply even when we're dealing with infants. Make sure you don't miss out on the courtesies when talking to them. Not only will it help them inculcate good habits, but they will feel great about themselves if treated well. When you say something to them, thank them for listening to you. When they do something out of the ordinary, make sure they know how good you felt. Our children help us with little odd jobs and are always so caring and considerate. They make us feel awesome. So why wouldn't we thank them often? Gratitude encourages them to respect you and themselves. And respect inspires love. Thank you is basically showing gratitude. And if we think about it, there are so many ways in which we probably don't even realize our children give us joy, for which we should be grateful. You can thank them for that amazing and adorable morning cuddle, for that cute smile, for trying to draw you a card, for helping you find something, for eating their meal so well, for making you smile, and for being a part of your life!

With you expressing this, they know they are appreciated, accepted, loved, and cherished, and that they get noticed when they do good deeds. And who doesn't like to be noticed? They will want to continue making you proud and in return expect only a gentle sign of appreciation. That isn't too tough, is it? Every action has an equal and opposite reaction, so if you value their behavior, they will do the same for you.

Be Happy Tips

1. Thank your children for the happiness and love they bring to your life.
2. Thank your children for listening to you.
3. Thank your children for helping you in small things.
4. Thank your children for the amazing hugs they give you, and the affection they show you, and tell them how much it means to you.
5. Thank your children for caring about you because as much as they are your world, you are theirs, and they give you love and adoration like no one else can.

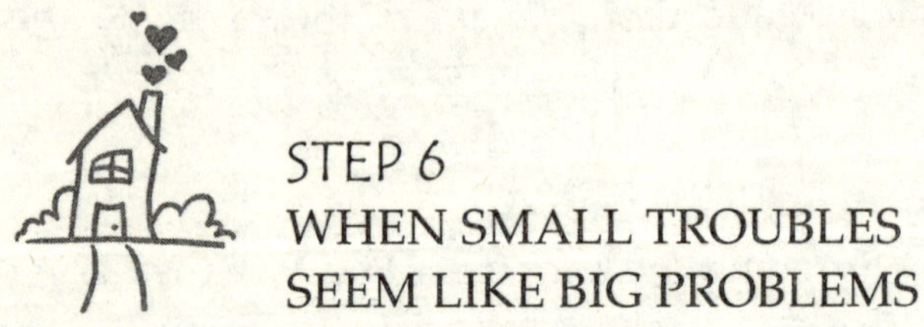

STEP 6
WHEN SMALL TROUBLES SEEM LIKE BIG PROBLEMS

FILTER THE WORLD

Outsiders, advice and judgment

Everyone seems to have a clear idea of how other people should lead their lives, but none about his or her own. ~ Paulo Coelho

Gone are the days when you'd have to be at least in your teens to be judged by people. I've heard four-year-olds being discussed for their 'chiseled' features, 'average' height, and 'impressive' manner of speaking. Seriously, can't children be left out of this when they're so young? To deal with these comparisons and comments, all you need to remember is that besides you and your child, no one else matters. Absolutely no one.

You know what's best for your baby, and don't let anyone's statements question that. Trust yourself. Hear outsiders' comments, take in the good parts and ignore all the negative things they have to say. Oh, and run away from competitive mothers who like comparing the growth and development of their child with yours. Those parents really will get to you beyond a point. As for the parents who are busy running the 'parent race', feel compassionate towards them. They are much too stressed and will only realize later that they did not truly enjoy their greatest gifts – their children. Here are some pointers to summarize my sentiments.

People will give advice

They think it's their duty to give you free advice. The best way to deal with those people is to continue listening to them quietly (if you have the patience), without indulging or encouraging what they have to say. If you know you will get irritated beyond a point, change the topic. Do remember that sometimes you can actually get some useful suggestions if you can filter the information and focus on the positives.

People will judge

People arc judgmental. That's probably one of life's great truths. So avoid meeting individuals who you know will have nothing good to add to your day. They will eventually ruin your mood. And really, they don't matter. You are an adult, and you connect with your child in a way that no one else can. At the end of the day, only you know what works best for your child.

Try not to judge others

Compassion and kindness are important traits in ourselves as well as in our children. We tend to think our way is the best or judge the ways of others. What we don't realize is that we can never ever truly know what someone else is going through or the reasons they make the choices they do. Everyone has many aspects to their lives that we don't know of, however close they might be to us. So when they make certain decisions or exhibit certain behaviors, instead of judging them, we must try empathizing with them. Think about it, aren't there so many things you juggle that an outsider or even a close family member may not be aware of? We may strongly believe someone is doing the wrong thing but usually we judge others about things that are really none of our business and about which we have half-baked or no information.

All parents devise their own methods of bringing up their children. And everyone's beliefs are correct in their own right. Sometimes it troubles me to see children being brought up by aggressive or suppressive parents. It would upset me initially. But then I realized that the phrase 'we are all victims of victims', is apt in this situation. There is a lot that goes into making parents what they are, including their own upbringing.

If we can, with love, share our insights with them, then we should. But if we can't, then we should not judge them for their way of life or be harsh towards them in any manner; that behaviour will only make them more defensive.

We cannot judge why others are too strict or too lenient with their children. We cannot know for sure why they make the choices they do regarding schools, upbringing, nutrition etc. We can never truly understand the situation of another person emotionally, financially, their support systems, family, and other pressures. No matter how well we think we know them, we can never know the full picture. So to judge their decisions would be unfair. Every parent loves their child deeply and tries their hardest to do their best, even if we don't see that sometimes.

So while we're developing our own parenting skills, let's also work on ourselves. Let's learn how to be there for those who could use a helping hand or a caring thought, without any judgment or negativity. Let us be kinder in our judgment of others and ourselves.

External judgments don't matter

There are two categories of moms you will come across – the over-involved mom and the under-involved mom. The children of both are happy, though their ways of dealing with their children are poles apart. However, they also have some attributes in common – they both judge the other kind and question themselves all the time. The over-involved mother derives satisfaction and a sense of worth from knowing that she is pursuing the path that is globally considered morally correct and acceptable. She puts her dreams aside, forgets her life, and focuses entirely on her child, which is commendable. But at the same time, she forgets that she too, needs to be taken care of, which is of equal importance, if not more so. Eventually, when the children leave the nest, she is at a loss to know what to do with her time. At the age of 45 or 50, when the children are settled and busy, what can she do with her life without any ambitions to pursue and no excitement or dreams? Do you want to be sitting by the phone waiting to hear from your children every moment of the day? I don't think so.

The under-involved mums, or as some call them, the 'weekend moms', are only considered under-involved by the over-involved moms. If she manages her professional and personal life within the same 24 hours, the over-involved mothers persecute her. Statements such as, 'Oh, she thinks earning money is more important than spending time with her children' and 'Why did she have a child if she didn't plan on giving it all her time?', will be frequently heard. On the other hand, working moms have their own share of issues with over-involved mothers. They believe that homemakers end up mollycoddling their children, don't give them space, and push too hard all the time. Tough to say who is right. Therefore, it is important to strike a balance in life and not judge others. We all need to do the best we can, as we know how.

Even 30 minutes of dedicated time spent with your child can be enough to form a beautiful and strong bond. Sometimes, during the day, when my son comes and gives me a long kiss on my cheek, I realize how true that statement is. Pure love and affection in tiny doses can do wonders for both parents and children. When at the end of a day I rest my back, my son sometimes surprises me by giving me a small massage, just as I give him a backrub when I put him to sleep.

Over-involved mums somehow always look down on under-involved moms and vice versa. And both look down on themselves too. They ask themselves whether they are doing enough, too much or too little. These are worries that have no correct answers. The only thing I would suggest, if you feel you fit into either of these categories, is quit looking for any acceptance. Do not compare yourself to any other mother. Unless you see someone implement a technique you feel would work well for your child as well, don't let worldly pressures get to you. All mothers try to give their children *the best they can*. You do too. And that really is more than good enough!

We can never judge the lives of others, because each person knows only their own pain and renunciation. It's one thing to feel that you are on the right path, but it's another to think that yours is the only path. ~ Paul Coelho

Surround yourself with positive people. Whether they are your closest childhood friends, pregnancy friends, school friends, heartbreak friends, or messiah-like friends, hang out with people who make you feel content and satisfied. Quit comparing yourself to others, unless you feel doing so in certain cases has a positive effect on your life and on your child's. Every mom tries her best; you do too. And that's good enough!

For instance, when my husband and I were encouraging my son to develop a taste for vegetables, we didn't want him exposed to too many chocolates and candy. At the time, a fair share of disagreements and comments came our way. People told me that my son loved chocolates all the more because I was denying him the pleasure of eating them. Some said, 'You deserve this. You've restricted him from eating something he loves.'

But I had never stopped him from playing with his remote-controlled toy cars. I did not ask him to not eat mushrooms, olives, or spinach. He loves them all. But because those who surround him have glorified chocolates, he has an innate weakness for them. And that's perfectly okay. It's natural for human beings to want to give into certain temptations. Remember, getting your children to adhere to these guidelines is not really the toughest part. The challenge comes when you try to ensure that even grandparents, friends, and other well-wishers, respect your decision and don't present the children with the temptation regularly. There will be lots of ups and downs at this stage. Sometimes you won't succeed, and that's okay. We can only try our best. And that's good enough!

People who want to judge you will find some reason or the other to do so. All you need to know is that you should do what you think is best, because it is the parents who think things through the most. I know many people pass comments on children who have working parents. They say that the children behave in a specific manner because their moms work. They blame the mothers for not imparting the right values and so on. Is there any research that has proven that children brought up by stay-at-home mothers are happier and more balanced than those whose moms are working? Or vice versa, for that matter? Not that I know of. What proves either right?

Yes, I have reiterated the importance of good advice in this book. It is true that it can be a great learning tool if filtered well. But for our own happiness, we must learn to consciously move away from negativity, adverse comments, and destructive suggestions. As a parent, you are the only one who has to decide what information you want to accept and what you don't. You have to compartmentalize your life and decide what fits into which category. Every method can be right. I have a simple manner of dealing with pessimistic people. Usually, if someone questions my beliefs, I make a run for it. I distance myself from such people, and if, God forbid, I am not in a situation to manage that, then I avoid having any conversations with them about parenting or my son. In fact, I never talk about my ideologies unless someone actively brings up the topic and is genuinely interested in knowing how I feel about something. But I must not discount the fact that I have also been blessed to meet parents who are on the same page as I am. They have been great sources of help and inspiration.

Since I strongly follow the 'don't give advice, until asked' philosophy in life, you might wonder what prompted me to write this book. Well, I did so because I had some thoughts I wanted to share with parents who are looking for solutions that actually work. And I have enumerated numerous such techniques. Many parents (and I), have implemented these methods in parenting and the results have been magical. Some you will know already and some will hopefully give you a new and better perspective. I also wanted to restore and strengthen the confidence of all fathers and mothers in their own abilities. They really do know what is best for their children.

Many modern young couples also believe that parenting is difficult. They sometimes decide against having kids because they 'want a life' after getting married and don't 'want to feel trapped'. Some also feel 'bringing up children involves too much work'. I want to erase this notion from all their minds and bring to the fore the joy of parenting. Sometimes, we parents are responsible for shaping such opinions. We tend to make others feel that being a parent is a full-time, relentless, and tiring job, by sharing our stresses regularly. Hence, we must also make the effort to relax and give ourselves time to let things fall into place. We too need some objectivity and de-stressing. Just continue doing your best, as you do, and leave the rest to the magic of the universe.

That way, we can encourage more people to experience the joy of having children. And we won't scare the younger generation into choosing not to do so. They too, need to know that they should not miss out on this absolutely amazing journey. Having a child does anything but restrict your growth. As a matter of fact, it helps you discover aspects of your personality that you did not know existed. The ecstasy of watching a soul that is part of you grow into a beautiful adult is beyond magical.

Be Happy Tips

1. Don't judge others. More importantly, don't care about what others have to say about you. Some people will always look at the glass as being half empty. That's how life is. We can't change that. But what we can do is stay away from

negative people, ignore their comments, and not give them any importance. If someone interferes or tries to negate your parenting philosophy, then distance yourself from that person. Situations like these only encourage conflict. You have the right to feel good about your abilities.

2. Continue loving your child in the best way you can. And know that doing so is enough. You are a great parent! No one has the right to question that; especially random people you bump into at parks and stores. No one knows the relationship your child and you share better than you do.
3. Don't always negate and shy away from advice. Take in the best and filter out what doesn't work for you. Sometimes you come across some really helpful suggestions from other parents who follow the same parenting philosophy and beliefs as you do.

GRANDPARENTS

Finding a balance

What children need most are the essentials that grandparents provide in abundance. They give unconditional love, kindness, patience, humor, comfort, lessons in life. And, most importantly, cookies. ~ Rudolph Giuliani

Often we hear how grandparents enjoy their grandchildren more than they did their children. The joy you see in grandparents interacting with their grandchildren is just another facet of the gift we are given in the form children. Grandparents have had their children and realized over the years the immense joy they bring. Also, most grandparents have a few regrets about not having spent enough time with their children, which they now want to redress with the next generation.

In addition, because of the natural progression of life, grandparents have more time on their hands as their work hours are fewer or they are retired. Grandparents come with great experience, great love for a new child, and time on their hands, so they can help out with the time-consuming experience. Many of us are blessed to have them interested in helping out and making things a lot easier for us. They are family and more trustworthy than any other to taking care of our children. We might want to work, travel, or just have a social life and time out. At such times, to have the option of leaving our children with them is a boon.

It doesn't come without its own difficulties, I agree. To begin with, maybe they don't want to be involved, and it hurts to know that they could help to make life so much easier for you, but they choose to not do so. Maybe they don't follow your parenting philosophies. They might have their own opinions on bringing up a child. Maybe they do things that they know you don't appreciate, or they like giving unsolicited advice or interfere. Maybe they over pamper and don't follow the boundaries you set. Yes, it could get messy. Since you are dealing with the life-changing experience of having a child, you are even more sensitive and prone to falling prey to upsetting thoughts. So I will put down a few thoughts which may make this confusing relationship a little easier.

1. You are lucky to have one or both sets of grandparents. The love your parents give you and your child is incomparable.

2. Every parent-child relationship has issues. Every parent-grandparent relationship has issues. In the best interest of everyone, we need to find solutions.
3. List the important areas of differences. Then mark which are critical and which are not so critical for you. Then work out how to resolve the critical issues.
4. Discuss and resolve things amicably. If grandparents insist on doing things their way, and if it is important to you that they do it differently, communicate this to them. Communicate with love and explain why certain things are important to you.
5. If things cross a line you are not comfortable with, lay the cards in front of the concerned people. Do so gently. Tell them that the child loves them and that you appreciate the amazing love they give. Tell them that they are an important part of the child's life, but it's *your* child and certain things are important to you. The rules will be yours, and if they want this relationship to continue, they must respect your decisions.
6. Try a few times. Then you can figure out whether the issues are still frustrating for you. If that is the case, you can take the call to distance yourself from them.
7. Remember a grandparent and child relationship is beautiful, and both sides benefit greatly. They are a great support system for you as a parent.
8. This will work if there is respect for the role of grandparents and at the same time respect for the decisions of parents.
9. Try to be flexible and focus on the core points that are important to you. Let the small things go.

I have some great memories of my grandparents during my childhood. They had time, patience, and calmness. And it's four more people to love you or your child! Think of how much your child will cherish that love. Plus, they have brought up your spouse or you, and you now know that wasn't easy. Every child will have some complaints about his/her childhood, and I'm sure you have yours. But in most cases you will realize when you become a parent that your parents were also young when they had you and like you, they did their best for their child.

All parents have limitations because they are human too. So forgive them, value them, and cherish them. If you work out these little issues, they can be a blessing. And if there are big issues that bring too much negativity into your life, then distance yourself from them. Figure out a better way to get the support you need. Yes, grandparents are amazing, but if it isn't working positively and you have tried your best, you need to find happiness in some other way.

Be Happy Tips

1. A grand parent can love your children with such depth and passion that they and you are lucky if you have them as a part of your lives.
2. Grandparents have brought up their children, hence you have come into the world and now have your own children. Value their role.
3. Grandparents don't have to give up their entire retired lives to help us. It is difficult enough for us to take care of our children but as one gets older, it's more tiring. So if they agree to take care of your child while you work or are away, be happy that you are lucky enough to have this support.
4. If, instead of being loving and supportive, they are negative or interfering, communicate to them the joy you are all missing out on. Hopefully they will realize, because with

age they see that family joys are more important than anything else in life.

5. If you still feel your parenting happiness is being compromised, take a stand. You know best as a parent; trust yourself and take the decision you feel works in the best interests of you and your child.

THE SECOND BIG DECISION

Schooling and academics ~ busting the stress

I've never let my school interfere with my education.
~ Mark Twain

Which school should I put my child into? Will my child get into a good school? Have I done my best? Is my child compromised because the neighbours have taken a different decision for their child's education? All of us have these questions. We all know people around us who are worried and stressed about the schooling question. At the same time, many children do not love going to school. Instead, they wake up nice and early on weekends but on school days they suddenly feel sleepy. Haven't we all loved the rainy days and snow days where we get unexpected holidays?

So I started to think about why we have schools. Is it to give moms a break? Is it to teach children how the human body works or the geography of the world? Is it to generally stimulate a child's mind? Is it to occupy children positively? Is it to instill some discipline or routine into a child's life? Different schools following different philosophies have different answers. Let's say it's actually all of the above. So don't all the schooling methods provide the above? In this day and age, all schools meet certain standards. Maybe some focus more on academics, others on sports or manners. Maybe you have a preference for one or the other. If so, great, go for the school that best fits your chosen criteria. Write a list based on what you think would make you and your child happy. If there is a race in your neighborhood for a particular school, and you want it too, okay try for it. But stressing about it really won't help. Tell yourself that in the long run, your child's happiness and success in life are not going to be determined by this. Think about it. Look around you. Do more successful people come out of a particular school or method? Aren't there many success stories about dropouts making it big and being happy and successful in life?

So do your best. Study your options, write a list of what you want and what your preferences are, and decide your plan of action accordingly. Now you have done your best. Leave the rest to the magic of your love for your child, to ensure that you are both happy.

In-house education

I remember reading that there are many types of intelligence. My focus has always been on three important categories that are usually ignored: emotional intelligence, spiritual intelligence, and social intelligence. Academic intelligence and physical intelligence are regularly addressed in our day-to-day lives.

With school admissions, interviews and intensive curriculums in schools, the development of academic intelligence is taken care of by our education system. Hence, I am not going to elaborate on that. However, there are a few essential aspects that I would like to share. Flash cards, for instance. Yes, if you use this technique actively, you can get your children to start reading by the age of four. But ask yourself, will it really determine how successful my child will be in life? Look around your world and you will have your answer.

What your child needs the most is active, positive, and respectful parenting. Children need your attention and love. Reading and learning will automatically follow. Enjoy, love, and respect your child. Everything else will fall into place without you needing to worry about it. Children's educational developments also differ as per the systems in various countries. In some parts of the world, children are not introduced to alphabets till the age of five or six. Whereas in other places, they could already be reading entire books by that time. There is no right or wrong way of going about this. Your child is learning every day. The best idea would be to follow the curriculum of the educational system/school your child attends. And go with the flow.

Instead of pushing children to excel at academics only, we should also focus on the other aspects mentioned in this book. Don't feel pressurized into believing that you need to do more or your child needs to work harder just because your neighbour's kid does. So what if you cannot boast how your child was reading at three? Does it matter whether he/she knows their arithmetic tables at the age of five? Not that much. But if you are positive around your children, and have instilled in them thoughts that will add to their spiritual and social intelligence, then what you will have is a happy child.

You will be proud to know that they are living each moment of their lives to the hilt and discovering their unique traits and talents every day. You will know that your children will be respectful, confident, good listeners and learners, open to change and to new cultures and cuisines, when they step out into the world. They will grow up to be positive human beings who will have all the 'real' traits and skills needed to lead a happy and successful life. However, there are some great techniques I have seen parents use to make learning fun and easy. A proactive atmosphere is one of the many things that helps.

Happiness tips to foster a creative environment for family learning

1. Follow the curriculum. Don't try to do 'more', just because your neighbours claims they do. Your child is perfect and a great learner in his/her own way.
2. Communicate with your child's teachers (only if you feel they aren't consistently negative). They spend a lot of time with your little ones, therefore they often have some good insights and tips to share.
3. Learn together. Spend time with your child, reading books on varied topics. This exercise not only helps builds his/her knowledge base, but also makes it a fun task to indulge in together.
4. Involve learning in daily activities. For example, introduce the custom of playing a dinnertime quiz game, where each person comes up with a question for the other. You can use this technique to introduce your children to a variety of topics without them feeling like they have been bogged down by the weight of thick books. And since it's a game, it will be welcomed.
5. Create a routine at the end of the day, when you discuss what your child's most interesting part or learning of their day was. This not only makes learning new things exciting, but also works as a revision exercise of sorts.

6. Question your children. Encourage them to think out-of-the-box. Try answering your child's question with another query. For instance, if he/she asks you why the water in the swimming pool is blue and why it isn't so when poured into a glass, give the child a chance to come up with an answer. Ask, 'Why do you think this is so?' Your child just might surprise you with the response. This helps children hone their analytical skills, something that will assist them in all their other educational endeavors as well.

BULLYING

Being singled out

When people see you're happy doing what you're doing, it sort of takes the power away from them to tease you about it.
~ Wendy Mass

Even though bullying has been an area of concern during our growing years, we have to also understand that it always has been a part of our lives. Bullying in the movies and on TV has always been there as long as the mediums themselves. The realities of bullying and the subconscious mind are controlled by what we have been exposed to. Explaining the effects of bullying or sidelining other children, and how it can hurt another child, is very important. Whether we can instill in our children a lateral belief towards equality is based upon our own behavioural examples and values.

On the other hand, we have to accept that our children will get exposed to bullying to some extent, and while it will break our hearts, it will help them to get tougher as well. So we should be there for them, protect them, but at the same time, not kill ourselves with worry about things that are a part of growing up. I went through a phase where I wanted to immediately step in whenever I saw my son's face drop if he was not asked to play with a group or when he was being physically pushed around. But as I stood there and gave him time to find his own response, he did. He stepped up for himself. It was better it happened in front of me rather than behind me. We also reaffirmed at home that how other children behaved was *their* decision. What was important was how *we* chose to act. He would discuss with us when a friend tried to hit him, and we would say that it was better if he kept his distance. By not overreacting, we made him realize it was a part of life and you can move on. It also made him realize that people are different. We don't want to learn the wrongs of other people; at the same time we can't control everyone. So we learn the good from others and stay away from the bad.

If you follow most of the above pointers and have good communication with your child, the chances are that you will know when he/she is experiencing bullying, and when it is getting out of hand and you need to intervene.

If your child is the perpetrator or is perhaps being influenced by other children into ridiculing another child, then talk to him/her with love and compassion. Ask if they would like to be spoken to like that and explain in a way they understand best, why we must never hurt another person, not only physically but also emotionally. Some comments from a child may sound funny to you but could break another child's heart. As parents, we can only be wish to see our children turn out to be responsible and sensitive to the feelings of others.

So maintain communication and build his/her self-confidence in every way you can, give the child lots of love and rest assured you don't have to worry too much about the bullies of the world.

Be Happy Tips

1. Accept that bullying is a part of life that many have to face. While you should be aware, you don't have to keep worrying about it.
2. Be observant, but give children time to find their own ground. The chances are they will. We all have pretty strong survival instincts.
3. Don't overreact when your child comes home with a story. Handle it calmly so he/she doesn't feel like it's the end of the world. How we react also determines how the child interprets the severity of a situation.
4. If you follow the tips here, you will have good communication with your child, which will give you clear signs of when the bullying is out of hand and needs personal/professional intervention.
5. It's important to let the child know that all sorts of people make up the world. What others do is their choice. What choices we make is what counts.

PEDIATRICIANS

The hunt for reliable advice

Trust yourself; you know more than you think you do.

~ Benjamin Spock

This is going to be the shortest section of this book. While our children's doctors are important, certain state checks, along with your own instincts, pretty much ensure fool proof protecting for our children. There are numerous resources online that are helpful but sometimes intimidating and confusing. I have also outlined a few things in this book such as envisioning positive things; ensuring your child eats a healthy diet with enough vegetable fibre, exposing your child to outside germs, which builds up immunity etc., that will help reduce your child's visits to the doctor. Speak to your gynecologist, neighbours and friends, and decide whom you are going to take your child to. Most doctors today don't pressurize the parents; it's just us who keep thinking nothing is good enough. So follow their instructions, and be happy! You're a great parent already.

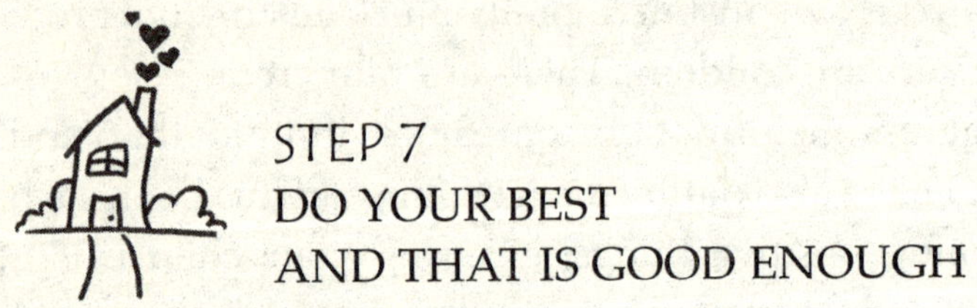

STEP 7
DO YOUR BEST AND THAT IS GOOD ENOUGH

You are a good parent. You have been wired by millions of years of evolution to fulfill your parenting obligations.

ME TIME

The trick to balance is to not make sacrificing important things become the norm. ~ Simon Sinek

Parenting is a magical and mind-blowing experience. All mothers and fathers adore their little ones. Sometimes, just running around with them is joyful in itself. You see the best in parents when they are with their kids. The love between them is the stuff fairy tales are made of. Even watching other parents is a truly magical and awe-inspiring experience. Sometimes it brings tears to my eyes when I see moms and dads involved with their children with utmost dedication.

Parents, to me, are like superheroes. Through thick and thin they are always there for their children. From when the little ones turn five days old, to the time when they are 50, children can always count on their parents' constant efforts to provide them with the best in life. For moms and dads, it is the single most satisfying job in the world. At the same time, it is not permanent. You're going to have to let your child fly off eventually. You don't want to be moping when that happens.

Also, in your day-today life, you don't want to be living your life only for and through your child. Hey, you're someone's child too, and you deserve as much fun as your child does. So take the time out for yourself – for hobbies, for work if you want, for date nights, for dancing, and for fun! Your child will only be the happier for it.

Babysitter dilemma

The pros and cons of having a babysitter, allowing breaks for parents, is an ongoing debate. But what is the true benefit of this. For parents to have a social life, meet friends and have occasional late nights, is good for the child as well as for the parents. Having a social life helps parents better accept and respect the responsibilities of having a child. I have seen parents who are so bound to their children that it creates dependence that may or may not be good. Hiring the right babysitter does involve you explaining to and making the sitter understand the kind of parent you are. Parents do look at the credentials of babysitters but what I believe gets missed is an explanation of your core parenting beliefs and parenting style. Do remember that a child does spend a good amount of quality time with a babysitter, so having your values explained and respected is quintessential.

Date nights

Time out for mom and dad together is important. When you are happy in your relationship as partners, it will spill over into your life's happiness quotient and help you be a happier parent. Working and going out is okay! Balancing parenting responsibilities with our responsibilities towards ourselves, is important.

Me time for mom and dad

We are responsible for ensuring we have time for what we enjoy. And if dad likes watching football sometimes, and mom likes getting pampered sometimes, you both need to support each other in enjoying these moments. And dads, if you think you cannot handle the child alone, or if moms worry that dads can't, here is the best news – *they can*! You just need to do it. Dads are just as capable as moms to take care of a child alone. In fact, if you leave them alone, they form an amazing bond. Once they get used to it, both the child and dad will look forward to their weekly jaunts with much excitement.

Be Happy Tips

1. Getting a babysitter (if affordable), or someone to help out, is fine. You don't have to dedicate every second of your life to your child. Do share your parenting philosophies with babysitter so there is consistency.
2. Date nights are great for parents. Connected parents make happier parents.
3. Do what you enjoy, just for yourself. Parents should support each other so both get to do what they love.

HUSBAND-WIFE RELATIONSHIP

Loving your partner

Don't worry that children never listen to you; worry that they are always watching you. ~ Robert Fulghum

The husband-wife relationship is so important. The more parents love each other, the more content and secure children will be. But how many couples can claim that? Not many. So it's okay. Yes, we all have complaints; the point is to realize that now there isn't just the two of you. You have someone else who is a part of the equation and who will find it hard to get over the fights, even if you do.

The most important thing a father can do for his children is to love their mother. ~ Theodore Hesburgh

So, though this is a book about parents and children, here are a few tips which can work wonders in a relationship.

1. You are equals, so respect each other as equals.
2. Be partners in happiness and sadness.
3. It's easy to be happy when things are good; try to be positive when they aren't.
4. When you don't have big problems, small problems seem big. Put things in perspective and see if they really are worth the fight.
5. Remember you got married to be together, for support, and security. Give each other that.
6. There are differences and there always will be, But that makes it much less boring.
7. Keep the sex alive, it's natural.
8. Make an effort to be groomed. Look good for each other.
9. Try to plan little surprises for each other.
10. Hug and enjoy the feeling of having someone hold you.
11. Try to relive and repeat the memories, holidays, and moments of the first years (the butterflies in your tummy moments).
12. Realize the joy in taking care of each other as a family. It's much more fun than most other things. Notice this.

SINGLE PARENTS

Accepting life as it is

Being a single parent is twice the work, twice the stress and twice the tears but also twice the hugs, twice the love and twice the pride.
~ Unknown

This section moves away a little from the positive focus, and if you are not in this situation, feel free to give this section a miss. So you have a child and no partner. This could happen during pregnancy, after delivery, or at a later stage. Whenever it does, it is equally tough. However, once it has happened, your options are to not have the baby or have the baby and put the baby up for adoption or have the baby and bring him/her up alone. Everything boils down to making a choice. Your choice. We need to realize that everything we do is our own choice. In the end, when you look at the core, the choice is always yours.

If you choose either of the first two options, do not feel guilty. Rather than bringing a child into the world and being miserable yourself, which in turn will lead to an unhappy child, it is absolutely okay to decide not to have the baby and wait till you are mentally and financially ready or desire to have a child. If you choose to put the child up for adoption, that's good too. There are so many couples who cannot have children but who are ready and crave this great experience. It is the toughest gift you can give someone but the biggest. You can have a child later when you are ready and able to enjoy the experience.

All three options are difficult. I spent many years trying to see logic in the ways of the world and why we get dealt certain cards in life. The conclusion I came to was that we come with certain baggage to this world. Some call it *karma* (the good and bad deeds of our previous and current lives). Some say our life is a reflection of us, a reflection of our thoughts (that our thoughts create how our life is today). I feel it's a mix of both. We are dealt certain cards based on some form of our past deeds. Then the work and thoughts we put in during this life, determine our lives in the future. While this is just a thought, we have to make the best of the choices we have today.

If you are in a difficult situation without a partner, you have to figure out practically what works for you. You have to decide whether you can work through the guilt/regret (though unnecessary) of the first two options, or whether you can handle the challenging job of bringing up a child alone. To help with this, I suggest the following.

1. Think about what works best in your situation long term. And I mean long term.
2. Don't live with guilt or regret. You are in a tough situation and obviously you didn't want to be in it.
3. Know that if you decide to bring up the child alone, it's more difficult than can image but also beautiful.
4. Your child will be fine. In the long run we all find some fault with our childhoods. If we don't have a *big* problem, we make small problems big. The child will might miss a second parent and go through phases of negativity, but who doesn't?

There are many aspects of this situation that I haven't covered. Parents in this situation will have hundreds of questions.

Post-separation, what's best for the child? But I am not going into that in detail as it is outside the scope of this particular book. The focus here is on the happiness of parents, the home environment, and happy, inspired children. This section is included so you understand these concepts also work in these situations and so that negatives can be put into perspective.

In the end, every situation is different. There is no right or wrong. Just take the decision that works best for you. Sometimes you find you are not single, but that only one parent is taking complete responsibility for the child. In that sense, he/she is a single parent. This could be the case because of situations at work or personal choice. It's a tough place to be in. But you will get through it. Parenting is a joyride with many ups and some downs. But in the end it's all worth it, and I hope you find the magic in the moments that will make it all worth it.

MOTHER KNOWS BEST

Trust your instincts

What good mothers and fathers instinctively feel like doing for their babies is usually best after all. ~ Benjamin Spock

Mothers have a super power that even doctors don't possess. Instinct allows moms to keep track of their children's health even when they aren't in front them. How does a mother know from the sound of her baby's cry that a diaper change is in order? How can she tell when her child is troubled? Instinct. Trust your gut feeling when it comes to situations you are unsure of or suspicious about. If your child is sick or you feel he/she is being bullied or hurt by someone, don't hesitate to act. Ask your kid what is wrong, and for all you know, you'll have averted trouble well in advance. Parents are intuitive. Mother nature has provided us with that gift so we can protect and nurture our children better. Here are a few instances that will reinstate your faith in yourself.

Instance 1

My sister-in-law has two children and is a fulltime, working mother. A few months ago, she was in the kitchen on the ground floor of her house, when she heard her four-month-old cry on the first floor. The baby was out of sight yet she instantly knew what was troubling her. She shouted out to her husband, "Check the diaper, she's uncomfortable". And the minute the diaper was changed, the baby stopped crying. This example is especially for those moms who beat themselves up for having a career and missing moments with their children. There's no such thing as a weekend mom. You may not be around your kid 24 hours a day, but you are always with him/her in thought and your instincts are always watching over your child, even when you don't know it.

Instance 2

This incident stuns me whenever I think about it. My sister was a thin child with no excess fat on her body. As a teenager, she suddenly began putting on weight. Thyroid issues weren't as common as they are now. Tests regarding it were also not part of general check-ups, specially not for children. My mom happened to have read about thyroid problems (her cousin had been diagnosed with it). Suspecting that to be the problem, she took my sister to the clinic. The doctors insisted my sister was completely normal and that the weight was baby fat. But my mom had a gut feeling she would not ignore. Deep down she knew something wasn't right and that the doctors were misdiagnosing her daughter's condition. She tried sharing her doubts with the doctors and even informed them that she felt it was a case of thyroid gland malfunction. But the doctors paid no heed. They dismissed her fears saying my sister was too young to develop thyroid issues. But my mom isn't one to give up easily. She went ahead and had the tests done, only to find she was absolutely right! All based on her gut feeling. My sister's condition wouldn't have been detected for many years if it had not been for my mother's strong instincts.

Instance 3

A close friend was going to a relative's house for dinner, but her son, for some reason, wasn't keen on going. She was surprised and felt something was amiss because usually he never refused to meet family members. To understand why he was uncomfortable, she sat him down and asked him why he didn't want to go. He told her that when this relative had come to their house earlier, she said something that he didn't like: "Why aren't you talking to me? If you won't spend time with me, then I will not talk to you again, and you can go away." The family member was an adult and knew that children needed to be given their space and not be bullied or blackmailed into listening. This wasn't the only thing that was upsetting the child. The last time this family member had visited, she kept asking him, "Who do you love more, your mom or your dad?" The child replied: "I love my mommy and my daddy". But the person tried to convince him to favor his father, saying: "When someone asks you that, you should always say your dad is nicer than your mom". There were other such comments from the person. Hence, he wanted to avoid visiting that family member.

The mom was glad she had figured out that something was troubling him. It was her instincts at work again. We shared laughs about maternal instinct later. She told her son that they knew he loved both parents equally. He learnt not to take some people in life seriously. It is true that children will meet many such individuals. Sometimes they may share the stories, and sometimes you may have to trust your instincts and figure out what's going on in their heads. Trust your own instincts, and you will always be there for your kids when they are hurt, to give them a platform to express themselves and to teach them how to handle these situations better.

Dear parents, I have always maintained that the tips in this book are meant for both fathers and mothers. Most also apply to all primary caretakers (nannies, grandparents, aunts, uncles). So, when I say 'mother knows best', I actually mean *parents* know best. I have seen so many dads who love and take care for their children in an amazing way. Children give them a sense of completion, and they spend a lot of quality time together. I have seen involved fathers who have great instincts too. They have their own ways of dealing and connecting with their children, and their efforts are admirable. For instance, my brother-in-law only needs to look at my niece's face to understand what she is thinking or feeling at that moment. He has a deep connection with her and his instincts strong.

Therefore, I want to say this as clearly as I can – fathers too, have great instincts. I have addressed this section to mothers because usually they are the primary caretakers and give their children more time as their top priority. This contributes to fine-tuning their instincts.

On the flip side, I also have male friends who are lovely people but who proudly announce they have been out with their friends for five days/nights in a particular week, while their wives sat at home and took care of their children. They take pride in doing so. But, we should try not to judge people. They may really enjoy that way of life. But they also miss out on the immense joys connected parents experiences. The happiness that bonding with your child brings is unparalleled, and Mother Nature or evolution has instilled instincts into our inner beings. All we have to do is trust our gut feelings and ourselves.

I believe becoming a parent is part of our natural progression. It's the way of Mother Nature – evolution, rebirth, and progress! Parenting is definitely not the arduous journey that it is made out to be. It is a blessing and is the most magical one in the world. I believe the joy is in the journey. I believe that in the end, it is all worth it!

Notes

Wish To Publish With Us?

We are always keen to look at interesting content across genres. Please email your submission to: **submissions@leadstartcorp.com**

The submission should include the following:

1. **Synopsis**
   A summary of the book in 500 - 1000 words. Please mention the word count of the manuscript.

2. **Sample chapters / Poetry**
   A couple of chapters from the book; these need not be in order, just send the best two chapters of the book. Or a few poems if the same is a collection of poetry.

3. **A Note About The Author**
   An interesting note about yourself (about 200 words).

4. **Additional Information**
   - Target audience
   - Unique selling proposition
   - List of illustrative content (if any)
   - Other comparative titles
   - Your thoughts on marketing the book